WATCH AND PRAY

By the same author:
Battle for Israel
Spiritual Character
The Uniqueness of Israel

Watch
and
Pray

Lance Lambert

KINGSWAY PUBLICATIONS
EASTBOURNE

Original transcript published by Christian Tape Ministry,
Richmond, Virginia, under the title *The School of Prayer*.
This edition first published 1995.

ISBN 0 85476 543 3

Designed and produced by
Bookprint Creative Services
P.O. Box 827, BN21 3YJ, England, for
KINGSWAY PUBLICATIONS LTD
Lottbridge Drove, Eastbourne, E Sussex BN23 6NT.
Printed in Great Britain

Contents

I

The Nature of Corporate Prayer

Again I say unto you, That if two of you shall agree on earth as touching any thing that they shall ask, it shall be done for them of my Father which is in heaven. For where two or three are gathered together in my name, there am I in the midst of them (Matthew 18:19–20).

And when thou prayest, thou shalt not be as the hypocrites are: for they love to pray standing in the synagogues and in the corners of the streets, that they may be seen of men. Verily I say unto you, They have their reward. But thou, when thou prayest, enter into thy closet, and when thou hast shut thy door, pray to thy Father which is in secret; and thy Father which seeth in secret shall reward thee openly. But when ye pray, use not vain repetitions, as the heathen do: for they think that they shall be heard for their much speaking. Be not ye therefore like unto them: for your Father knoweth what things ye have need of, before ye ask him. After this manner therefore pray ye: Our Father which art in heaven, Hallowed be thy name. Thy kingdom come. Thy will be done in earth, as it is in heaven. Give us this day our daily bread. And forgive us our debts, as we forgive our debtors. And lead us not into temptation, but deliver us from evil: For thine is the kingdom, and the power, and the glory, for ever. Amen. For if ye forgive men their trespasses, your heavenly Father will also forgive you: But if ye forgive

*not men their trespasses, neither will your Father forgive
your trespasses* (Matthew 6:5–15).

*I exhort therefore, that, first of all, supplications, prayers,
intercessions, and giving of thanks, be made for all men; For
kings, and for all that are in authority; that we may lead a
quiet and peaceable life in all godliness and honesty. For this
is good and acceptable in the sight of God our Saviour; Who
will have all men to be saved, and to come unto the knowledge of the truth* (1 Timothy 2:1–4).

*And being let go, they went to their own company, and
reported all that the chief priests and elders had said unto
them. And when they heard that, they lifted up their voice to
God with one accord, and said, Lord, thou art God, which
hast made heaven, and earth, and the sea, and all that in
them is: Who by the mouth of thy servant David hast said,
Why did the heathen rage, and the people imagine vain
things? The kings of the earth stood up, and the rulers
were gathered together against the Lord, and against his
Christ. For of a truth against thy holy child Jesus, whom
thou hast anointed, both Herod, and Pontius Pilate, with the
Gentiles, and the people of Israel, were gathered together,
For to do whatsoever thy hand and thy counsel determined
before to be done. And now, Lord, behold their threatenings:
and grant unto thy servants, that with all boldness they may
speak thy word, By stretching forth thine hand to heal; and
that signs and wonders may be done by the name of thy holy
child Jesus. And when they had prayed, the place was shaken
where they were assembled together; and they were all filled
with the Holy Ghost, and they spake the word of God with
boldness* (Acts 4:23–31).

This book does not deal with private or personal prayer
but with corporate prayer; and although I shall make
references to private prayer now and again, they will be
few. I will be confining myself to this subject of corporate
prayer that is so little understood and so little taught. It

seems that it is almost a lost art. For example, there are hardly any books written on corporate prayer. There are a multitude of books on personal prayer and private devotion, but I know of only two books on corporate prayer. One is Arthur Wallis's *Pray in the Spirit*; and even that is more personal than corporate. And there is the book of Watchman Nee's ministry, *The Prayer Ministry of the Church*. This is a very simple but clear book on corporate prayer, and I strongly recommend it.

Another valuable book which illustrates the principles of corporate prayer is the biography of Rees Howells: *Rees Howells, Intercessor*.

It is a very sad fact that one can count on the fingers of one hand the groups (including charismatics) that really know how to pray. There are lots of prayer meetings; but there are very, very few groups who really know how to pray together and how to pray a matter through together. The powers of darkness have worked so insidiously that many prayer meetings are anything but meetings for prayer. Sometimes they are tacked on to the end of a Bible study. (Alan Redpath used to say, years ago, that if you have the Bible study and the prayer meeting on the same night, you get neither a proper Bible study nor a proper prayer meeting.) Sometimes, it is just ten minutes on the end of an evening. Other times, at the so-called prayer meeting, a tremendous amount of information is given, and at the end about ten or twelve minutes are spent in prayer. There are the united prayer meetings—a week of prayer when, every evening, we are given forty-five to fifty minutes of ministry; and at the end of it, about ten to fifteen minutes of prayer.

Whole groups of God's people are paralysed or blockaded and the work of God is rendered very largely ineffective. For whether we like it or not, God's word tells us that we wrestle not against flesh and blood, but against

principalities, against powers, against the world-rulers of
this darkness, against hosts of wicked spirits in the
heavenly places. We are told to take to us the whole
armour of God and, having done all, to stand. And we
are to take the sword of the Spirit and we are to pray at all
seasons with all prayer and supplication in the Spirit (see
Ephesians 6:10–18).

So often, we think we are only up against flesh and
blood. We see the apathy of the neighbourhood. We see
the indifference of the people around us. We see a kind of
hardness coming into all evangelistic outreach. We may
have some difficult Christians who appear to block everything. It is always flesh and blood. It is either the brother
who is leading or someone else in the congregation or
group who has gone wrong in some way. Now, of course,
the enemy uses flesh and blood; but the word of God says,
'We wrestle not against flesh and blood, but against principalities, against powers, against the world-rulers of this
darkness, against hosts of wicked spirits in the heavenly
places.'

What does this mean? It means that behind flesh and
blood, behind ideologies, behind new philosophies,
behind new current ideas, there are spiritual powers that
are ruling the present spiritual darkness and holding in
their captivity thousands of people. A whole community
can be kept in bondage. A local church can be subjected to
a blockade and finally paralysed and sat upon by the
enemy; and if those dear children of God do not wake
up, the enemy will sit on them until all life is smothered.

After all, the apostle Paul did not say, 'We are in a
tennis championship with Satan.' He said, 'We *wrestle*
against principalities, against powers, against the world-
rulers of this darkness.' Now wrestling is not a polite
sport. It is not just some sort of game where you send a
ball back and forth, back and forth, back and forth; and

you mark up the points. 'Ah well, we have done well today; the enemy is gone.' The apostle Paul did not use a polite sport to illustrate his point. He used a sport that is impolite, something that is sweat and blood and means that you may have your arm twisted up your back or your leg nearly torn off; or you may be flung to the other side of the ring and the next moment have some heavyweight sitting on you.

Many Christians think that it should all be a joy ride, that we believers should have a wonderful, bubbling experience all the time; and if there is any sense of the enemy's presence, then something must be wrong. But the fact is that there are times when those powers, those world-rulers of darkness, those hosts of wicked spirits are going to get us into a vice-like grip. There are times when they will sit on us. But if you have ever watched a wrestling match, you know that just because some heavyweight is sitting on another heavyweight, it does not mean that he has won the match. The one underneath may get up and go on to win the whole match.

So what does it mean to wrestle with these powers? Surely it means that, somewhere, there has to be a prayer ministry. Before we can see a community broken open to the power of God and to the working of God, some have got to get behind the scenes and paralyse the enemy. Our Lord said, 'First bind the strong man if you would spoil him of his goods.' But we never think of that. We think that as long as a person preaches long enough, someone is bound to get saved. As long as you get a well-run evangelistic meeting, as long as you have the right sort of atmosphere, people are sure to be set free. But you can have all those things and still be up against a brick wall. The more vital and the more spiritually valuable any work is, the more likely it is that the enemy will come right in and sit on it. He does not just stand back and let you have a good time if there is any chance that there is going to be a permanent breakthrough.

So we have to understand this very simple fact: there can be little more strategically vital to the church of God than this matter of corporate prayer. In the days that lie ahead, during the last phase of world history, we shall need to know how to pray together and how to pray a matter through together. Furthermore, should real persecution come in the decades that lie ahead and should we lose our liberty, then we have got to know how we can break through together. It is no good waiting until that day dawns to think, 'Now what did they say years ago in that school of prayer? What were we always being taught?' It will be too late! When that day dawns, the enemy will also have far greater power. You will not be able just to go and study some book and work up, as it were, all the principles of corporate prayer. Unless the Spirit of God has burned it into us, we shall be found lacking in the day of our crisis.

That is why it is so necessary—for new Christians as well as those of us who are older in the Lord—to learn the lesson, however costly it is to us. Some of us older ones have learned such bad habits in prayer that they have become second nature to us. But it is no good throwing in the sponge and saying, 'Oh well, it is too late for me to try to learn new things now.' Do you mean to tell me that the Holy Spirit cannot overcome your background? He can keep all that is best and most valuable of your background and he can overcome all the bad things—if you will only trust him, if you will only be open to correction. The basis of all learning is to be meek. The moment a person says, 'I do not need that,' that person ceases to learn.

I don't want you just to swallow everything I say. I want you to take it right back to the Lord and sort it out. I believe that we must learn how to use this colossally effective weapon which God has placed into the hands of his church.

Four kinds of prayer

In 1 Timothy 2:1, we find four kinds of prayer which comprehend all the aspects of prayer. It is interesting that each of these four words is used in the plural: supplications, prayers, intercessions and thanksgivings.

Supplications

The word *supplications* primarily means 'a need'. The Authorized Version, the Revised Version, the American Standard Version, and the Revised Standard Version all use the word 'supplications'. The New American Standard Bible uses the word 'entreaties'. We are talking here about asking or entreating or beseeching. There is a sense of need and earnestness in asking or appealing because of that need. This is not just asking something of God—it is an earnest appeal to God.

Why is so much prayer ineffectual? Why is it that, so often, after a prayer meeting we come out of it and have to try and convince ourselves we have done some good? We say, 'Now of course God does hear prayer.' Something deep inside us seems to say that most of what happened did not go above the ceiling. And that happens when we are praying our own prayers, when we have not stopped to enquire of the Lord. Unless we supplicate the Lord, unless we enquire of him, unless we appeal to him on the basis of this urgent need, we shall never know his mind about it. And because we do not know his mind, we shall be threshing around in prayer, using many words and getting nowhere.

Enquiry of the Lord is fundamental to all prayer. We cannot pray aright, we cannot use the weapons provided

unless we first know the Lord's mind on the matter. Only
when we have the Lord's word, only when we have
enquired of the Lord, will we have the sword of the Spirit
which is the word of God. Then we won't have to play
around. We won't have to spend half an hour making
noises or saying all sorts of lovely scriptural phrases
which don't mean anything. We will have the word of
the Lord.

Sometimes the Lord will give that word to one person
and we only need to rise up and take that word once it has
come. The Holy Spirit will give insight into that word to
one person after another, and we should be able to pray
through that whole situation with that word from God. It is
the sword of the Spirit that cuts right through the problem.

We need to enquire of the Lord about healing. We need
to enquire of him about other matters, such as practical
provision. It is no good saying, 'It says in the word of
God, "We have not because we ask not," therefore I am
going to ask the Lord for a Rolls Royce.' Many people
have had terrible disappointments because they reasoned
like that. They have asked the Lord for all kinds of things,
and when their prayers are not answered they feel the Lord
has let them down or there is something wrong with them.
They feel that they are not in the inner circle of God's
'special ones' because they don't see anything happen.

The fact is that you cannot just take any scripture and
batter it into being. You have to enquire of the Lord; and
only when you have clearly in your heart and your spirit
that God says, 'Yes, yes,' can you go ahead. That is what
it means when it says, 'If you ask and do not doubt in your
heart, you shall have what you ask.' You may have many a
doubt in your mind, but you do not doubt in your heart.

This matter of supplication is absolutely fundamental. I
do not think there is anything more important than to
underline this matter of supplication. It is the missing

link. The Lord will not keep you waiting night after night. He only waits for us to come to him with an enquiring attitude and then he will say, 'Here it is.' We have got the idea that the Lord is like us, that he has to be cajoled and humoured and nursed into a nice mood. Then when he is in that sweet mood, we can get out of him what we want. But the Lord is not like that. He is more interested in touching people's lives than we are. He is more interested in certain situations than we are. He only wants a spirit of enquiry and then, sometimes almost immediately, he will give clearly the direction. Don't go at prayer like a bull in a china shop, or like a tank mowing everything down. Simply ask: What is the Lord's mind on this matter? How are we to pray? What is the word God would give us? What is the right weapon to use?

Prayers

The second word is *prayers*. This is the most frequently used term in the New Testament and is the general word for prayer. Literally, it means 'pouring out'. That is what prayer is—a pouring out. You pour out all the need; you pour out all the hurt; you pour out all the feeling. That is prayer. I think most of us understand that and don't need to spend longer on it.

Intercessions

The third word is *intercessions*. The word used here carries the idea of petitioning a superior—a king, a magistrate, a prince—someone with authority. That is probably why the New American Standard Bible uses the word 'petitions' instead of 'intercessions'. The idea is of petitioning someone who has the authority to do something. We are seeking the presence and hearing of

God on behalf of others or for situations in which we are all involved. That is intercession.

In some ways this is the deepest aspect of prayer and the least experienced. There are very few of God's people who know much about corporate intercession. Why? Because intercession is not just a few words mouthed on behalf of someone else, but should involve our spirit, our soul, and our body. If you would be an intercessor, look out; for God will require every single thing that belongs to you—spirit, soul, body, time, energy, health, possessions. God will take everything. Never devalue the word intercessor.

I don't want you to be frightened by this. Don't say, 'Now I am not going to do anything any more. I will have to take my name off the Intercessors for Britain list and a few other things. You really frighten me to death with what you have said about intercession.' We all have to start somewhere, and God loves a person who is ready to intercede. I believe that you come nearer to the heart of God when you are prepared to be an intercessor than in anything else you do. And if you are prepared to be an intercessor, God will lead you step by step—first from the kindergarten of intercession into the preparatory school and then on into high school and university. Do not ever think that intercession is easy.

When you are young in the Lord and you say, 'Lord, I want to intercede,' God will give you the matters that you can handle. But he longs for those with the spiritual capacity or maturity who can really intercede on matters that are vital to his purpose in this world.

Thanksgivings

Thanksgiving is the giving of thanks not only for answered prayer but for the Lord himself. Most people think immediately of thanksgiving as thanking the Lord for the prayers we asked of him last week that have been answered in between. But the Bible says, 'Let your requests be made known unto God with thanksgiving.' Do you understand that? You may have a request, so you say to the Lord, 'Lord, here is my need. Would you please do so and so about it, and I want to thank you now for the answer.' I believe that is to devalue the word 'thanksgivings'.

It is not just that we thank God that he is going to answer or that he has answered. The important thing is the giving of thanks for what God is, and for all that he is. We give thanks for his grace, his love, his mercy, his throne, his truth. This whole matter of worship—which is such a vital and strategic part of corporate prayer—is involved in this word 'thanksgiving'.

Many of us are so self-centred that the enemy can just twist us around his little finger. He comes to us and says, 'Now it is no good for you to worship the Lord; you have been in a bad mood all day. The children were badly behaved, and the office was awful because the boss gave you too much to do. You had a dreadful journey home from work and you are in a ratty mood. It is no good you thanking the Lord. You are just a failure.' And you say, 'Of course, the one thing I want is to be real. I do not want to be a hypocrite. I will not open my mouth and praise the Lord and thank the Lord when I am just being a hypocrite.' And the devil says, 'Of course not. Absolutely. You do not want to be a hypocrite. Better not try to worship God today.'

The enemy has now got you into a position where you can only praise the Lord when you feel good. The devil's whole machine will be geared up to making sure you feel bad because he wants to destroy any thanksgiving or any worship. He knows that worship and thanksgiving and praise are tremendous weapons in the battle that we are in. We so often fall for this line of the enemy hook, line, and sinker. Sometimes, people will go for years without even opening their mouth and praising the Lord. They cannot even bring themselves to tell him that he is lovely. They cannot proclaim that his throne is for ever.

But we must realise that we can be honest with God. We can say, 'Lord, I feel awful. I had a dreadful day today, but I thank you, Lord, that your throne is the same. My having an awful day has not brought about an abdication in heaven.' The idea seems to be that if we get out of bed on the wrong side, there has been a crisis in heaven. If we have eaten something at night which did not agree with us and we wake up with a rather jaundiced view of things, the Lord has abdicated. But that is nonsense. When you are down, you can praise the Lord; and when you are up, you can praise the Lord. Now when you are down you can be honest. You can say, 'Lord, I do feel dreadful, but I want to thank you for what you are. You are wonderful. You are just simply marvellous. All your works are wonderful. Your truth lasts for ever. Just at present, I have got a rather jaundiced view of things, Lord, but above my jaundiced view, your truth is for ever.'

And then what will the devil say? 'This person is talking truth; now what do I do? I cannot do anything.' So he says to his whole hierarchy: 'Leave so and so alone for a while. More value comes out of him when he is having a bad time than when he is having a good time.' Some of you are helping the enemy to keep you in a permanent bad time because you have not learned this lesson: I will bless the Lord at all times. When we say to the Lord, 'Thank you so much, my heart is bubbling over with joy. I am full of peace. I feel absolutely marvellous,' we are not blessing the Lord, we are blessing ourselves. We are simply saying all that *we* are. But if we just forget ourselves and bless the

Lord then we will find that the joy will come back into our hearts, the peace will come back into our lives.

It is so wonderful when we see that we can bless the Lord at all times and his praise—*his praise*—is continually in our mouth. Then we have a weapon in our hand. It says, 'The high praises of God in our mouths and a sharp two-edged sword in our hands.'

The principle of corporate prayer

> *Again I say unto you, That if two of you shall agree on earth as touching any thing that they shall ask, it shall be done for them of my Father which is in heaven. For where two or three are gathered together in my name, there am I in the midst of them* (Matthew 18:19–20).

The principle of corporate prayer is togetherness, or to use another word, 'mutuality'.

Consider the word 'agree': 'Again I say unto you, that if two of you shall *agree* on earth as touching anything that they shall ask, it shall be done for them of my Father which is in heaven.' Now this word 'agree' is from the Greek word *sumphoneo* from which we get our English word *symphony*. It really means, literally, to sound together, to harmonise together. It was primarily used of musical instruments.

It is the word we get in the story of the prodigal son when he came home and heard the sound of music. He heard a *sumphoneo*. It is also the word which occurs in 2 Corinthians 6:16: 'What agreement [concord] hath an idol with the temple of God?' Here again the thought is of musical instruments blending and harmonising together.

Now often when we think of this verse, Matthew 18:19, we think it means that we agree to agree. By agreeing to agree, we think we can twist the arm of God and get him to do something which he is basically unwilling to do. He

does not really want to do it, but if you and I agree, we can
twist his arm and get it out of him. Now that is putting it
very crudely, but that is exactly the idea that is so prevalent about this verse. We agree to agree and God, who
really does not want to do this thing, will have to do it.
The whole thing is a lie. Why? Because of this little word
for.

I have heard many sermons on the first sentence: 'Again
I say unto you, that if two of you shall agree on earth as
touching anything that they shall ask, it shall be done for
them of my Father who is in heaven.' And I have heard
many sermons on the second sentence in verse 20: 'For
where two or three are gathered together in my name,
there am I in the midst.' But I have hardly ever heard a
message on the real meaning in these two verses.

Look at it: 'Again I say unto you, that if two of you shall
agree on earth as touching anything that they shall ask, it
shall be done for them of my Father who is in heaven. *For*
where two or three are gathered together in my name,
there am I in the midst of them.' Now that 'For' means
that the second sentence qualifies the first. The whole first
sentence has got to be understood in the light of the
second sentence. What does this mean? It means simply
that where two or three are gathered together in the name
of our Lord Jesus, he is there; and because he is there in
their midst, he gives expression to his mind and will and
purpose which will be evident in the midst of the members
of his body. There will be agreement.

And what is the significance of being gathered in the
name of our Lord? Is that name just a little charm that we
end our prayers with? 'In the name of Jesus' is not a
wrong way to end your prayer, but what do you mean
by it? Are you using it as a kind of little magic formula?
What we mean is: 'Father, we are one with your Son; we
are joined to him; he is the Head, we are the body. In the

name of the Head, we are gathered.' Now we begin to
understand. It is a question of our position. We are joined
to the Lord. We are members of his body. He is in our
midst. We are in him and he is in us.

When we begin to see this, we find something very
wonderful. We find Christ's presence in the midst of
us—the Spirit of God leading, directing, prompting,
enabling. And so the prayer time becomes an expression
of the body of Christ, an expression of our oneness *with*
Christ and our oneness *in* Christ.

Sometimes when Christians meet together the prayers
that are offered are just totally individualistic. They have
no regard to the body of Christ. There is no 'harmonising'
with others. One would almost think the person praying
has not heard anyone who has prayed before and will not
hear anyone who comes after. It is a totally unrelated,
individualistic type of prayer. There is nothing wrong
with that when we are on our own, but when we are
together, it is a denial and contradiction of the very
principle of corporate prayer, which is: 'For where two
or three are gathered together in my name, there am I in
the midst of them bringing about agreement.'

Real agreement is when we are gathered together in the
name of our Lord, and when we take our position in
Christ—one body in Christ. We wait on him, we enquire
of him, we entreat him. And into our midst comes the
mind of the Lord. And it does not need long prayer.
Sometimes, it will come as someone prays: something
kindles in your heart and you know as you hear them
praying: 'Oh yes, that is right.' You can hardly wait for
them to stop. I sometimes wish we could do what it says in
the Scripture—that if one prophet is speaking and a
second has a revelation, let the first shut up. When a
burden comes into your heart it is terrible when someone
prays too long. When it is really corporate prayer, it is the

Holy Spirit who goes from one to the other. If someone prays too long, that prompting may be lost. The thing that will establish agreement among us is the fact that it is in the mouth of two witnesses at least. Why does God need this agreement? I do not know. All I know is that God is not unwilling to do this or that or the other. He wants to do it; but once we are in line with him, he wants that agreement expressed in the mouth of at least two witnesses.

We feel so often that if one person has prayed for something, that is enough. But on important matters we need to learn the lesson of agreement. Sometimes, the anointing of the Spirit will stay on something and thirty people will pray the same thing—like going around Jericho—again and again and again and again until the walls fall down. Another time, it only needs two or three people and the thing is done, and the anointing moves on.

This is the great distinguishing mark of the New Covenant. Under the Old Covenant everyone prayed together. They all prayed their own prayers and God sorted it all out in heaven. There was no relatedness to one another. They were absolutely saved—just as you and I are—redeemed by the blood of the Lamb, looking forward to the cross— but they were individuals. The great distinguishing mark of the New Covenant is that God has put his Spirit within us and we are no longer individuals; we are members of a body.

That was the thing that bowled over the Jewish people in the early days of the Christian church. They could not understand it. What was it with these people? They moved together as if some invisible conductor was there. One came in, then another one, then another, then another, and the place was shaken. It was not just a congregation of units; it was a body in Christ joined to the Head, in him, and under the direction and the government of the Holy Spirit.

If prayer is just so many individual units praying without too much regard to one another, then we might as well suggest matters for prayer and send everyone home to pray alone. This would cut the wastage of time by about seventy-five per cent. If everyone is going to pray their own prayers, just as if no one else is there, why don't we give out all the matters for prayer, which would take about half an hour, and then send everyone home to spend ten minutes on their knees in the quiet of their own room? Think of all the time we would save!

We all know what prayer meetings are like. When the first person prays, maybe he prays for some Billy Graham campaign in Los Angeles. Then he prays for a family in great need in Cape Town. Then he is off to Melbourne where there is a brother who has gone away from the Lord. Then he goes to Tokyo and prays for Shugaru. Then he goes back to London and prays for a group there. Then he prays for Grandmother's gangrenous toe. That is his prayer.

Then the next person comes in. He prays for this fellow in Melbourne who has gone away from the Lord. He goes to Shugaru in Japan. He comes back to Billy Graham in Los Angeles. He goes to London and he prays fervently for London and the British people. Then someone over in the back prays. He prays for the grandmother's gangrenous toe and for five other sick people. Then he prays for Billy Graham in Los Angeles. Then he has gone off to Melbourne. Then he goes to Tokyo for Shugaru and finishes there. Then someone else comes in and prays for Shugaru in Tokyo. He hops across to Peking and prays for all the saints behind the bamboo curtain. He goes off to Russia and prays for all the saints behind the iron curtain. He then ends in the Czech Republic, fervently praying for those who received the gospel out-reach sheet. Then someone over here prays for all those who are suffering everywhere, especially in the benighted Catholic countries. Then he is back to the iron curtain; and from the iron curtain, he is off to Tokyo.

What is happening in this prayer meeting? First, we are here, then we are there, then we are somewhere else. We go backwards and forwards, backwards and forwards. If you prayed like that at home, the Lord would say that you needed some help. When you pray at home, you get on your knees and you pray for Billy Graham, shall we say, and his campaign in Los Angeles. Then you go on to this matter in Melbourne, then you go on to Shugaru in Japan, and maybe you go to Cape Town in South Africa, and finally, you pray for some of the local needs. You don't dodge backwards and forwards between all these things. If you did, the Lord would say, 'My child, you need healing of the mind. You are all over the place.'

But in the corporate time, that is exactly what we do. We go all over the place and get nowhere. The edge is blunted, and we do not know where we are going. An evidence of this kind of prayer in many, many places is the use of 'I' and 'my'. Now there is nothing wrong in saying 'me' when you mean 'me' and saying 'I' when you mean 'I'. Some people say, 'Lord, we *all* feel so dead.' We cannot witness to that kind of thing. I do not feel dead. But they say, 'We *all* feel dead.' I say, 'Lord, count me out. I do not feel dead.' That brother or that sister should say, 'Lord, I feel so dead. Help me, Lord.' And maybe some others would take up that prayer and say, 'Lord, we pray for our brother.' Be honest.

But it is sad when you get too much 'I' and 'my' and 'me' in a time of corporate prayer. Our Lord never taught us this. He taught us to pray, '*Our* Father, who art in heaven, hallowed be thy name. Thy kingdom come. Thy will be done, as in heaven, so on earth. Give *us* this day our daily bread. Forgive *us* our debts, as *we* forgive our debtors. Lead *us* not into temptation, but deliver *us* from evil.' It is all in the plural. It is 'we', 'us', 'our'; and that is a sign that we really feel we belong to the body, where we can begin to pray in the name of the body.

The right kind of prayer time has an order and a design and a togetherness and a harmony. If our Lord is in the midst and, by his Spirit, is showing us his mind, there will be a purpose and an end and a design and a harmony and a togetherness in that time. We will never be perfect. The best of us will get it wrong at times; but nevertheless we should be seeing the design and the harmony.

The seconding of one another's prayers is so important here. You do not have to be a great saint or to have lived years and years in the service of God to distinguish an anointing on someone in prayer. You listen to a person and you know that the anointing is there. There is a clarity, there is an authority while they are praying. And so often we think, 'That is enough; we do not have to do any more about that.' However, it must be seconded—'If two of you shall agree. . . .' Sometimes, and I know this sounds a bit irreverent, I wish that people would just say, 'Lord, I second that.' It would be worth a thousand other words just to hear them claim agreement in that way.

This word 'Amen' is so interesting because it comes from the same root as the Hebrew word *aman*, which simply means 'to believe', 'to have faith'. When you say, 'Amen,' what you are saying is: 'I believe; I have faith for that, Lord.' Think about that the next time someone is praying and God puts into your heart a witness that it is right. Just say, 'Amen. I have faith for that; I am with that; I am right behind that.'

That is exactly what it means in 1 Corinthians 14:16, when it says, 'How shall the unlearned say "Amen"?'

There must be an awful lot of unlearned in some meetings because in some meetings I go to no one ever says 'Amen'. The word 'unlearned' in the Greek means 'the person without gifts'; it does not mean the unbeliever. Even the person who has not yet had his gifts manifested can say 'Amen' when they hear a gift—in this case prophecy, of course—being exercised. They can understand it and then they can say, 'Amen. Even so.'

A time of prayer should be conducted like a military operation. The idea seems to be prevalent among believers that as long as you have a gun and enough ammunition, you just keep firing—that is all that matters. Aiming your sight on the enemy and firing accurately is a very secondary thing. The idea is that the devil is so dimwitted that all we have to do is make a hullabaloo, shoot off a few scriptures in different directions, make a noise here and there, have lots of people saying prayers in the name of Jesus, and the devil will just run away.

The fact of the matter is that we are in a warfare and that the weapons of our warfare are not of the flesh but of God. We for our part have got to train our weapons or our guns on to the target.

Things to avoid in prayer

Now that leads me to a few practical points on corporate prayer. There are a number of things that we need to avoid like the plague.

Horizontal prayer

All prayer should be vertical. Avoid horizontal prayer, which is simply information giving, and is for one another's attention. Just be honest and break in and say, 'I ought to mention this. There is Mrs So and So round the corner in the Vineyard, number so and so on the third floor in the back room. Her husband fell down the other day and broke his leg, her child is in hospital with diphtheria, and she is in dreadful need. Could we pray for her?' So often we turn all this into 'prayer': 'Oh Lord, we pray for Mrs So and So who lives on one of the roads off Halford Road, the Vineyard, number so and so, third floor up and in the back room. Her husband has broken his leg and the child is in hospital with diphtheria.' The Lord knows all this, and when we fall into this error we are not praying.

How will you feel when you get to heaven and say, 'I did pray,' and the Lord replies: 'You did not. You spent most of your time giving information to others. Your prayers were a lot of hot air and as far as we are concerned in heaven, you were a dreadful bore. You destroyed those prayer meetings. Why didn't you learn? Why didn't you allow me to do something with you?'

Horizontal prayer is a plague. Ask God to keep you free from it. All prayer should be directed to God. God knows. That is why the preacher said, 'Remember, God is in heaven and thou on earth; therefore, let your words be few.' He did not mean don't pray much. He meant that God knows it all.

What did our Lord say? 'Do not use vain repetitions. Do not pray long prayers like the Gentiles who think for their much speaking they are heard of God.' He said, 'Remember, your heavenly Father knoweth what you have need of before you ask him.' It does not mean that we are not to ask, for he taught us to pray: 'Give us this day our daily bread.' But he said: 'Do not go all around the bush. Your heavenly Father knows it anyway. Be direct.'

Sermonettes

Then there are the little sermons and the Bible outlines. Our dear Lord is more preached at than any other person

in the whole universe. If the heathen were preached at as
much as the Lord, some things might be different. People
will give a rehash of the Sermon on the Mount or some
other scripture. The trouble is that the prayer meeting is
often the venue for frustrated preachers. It cannot get out
anywhere else so out it comes in prayer. We have biblical
outlines and points one, two, three, and four—and all the
points beginning with the same letter. May the Lord
preserve us from sermonettes. There is a place for rehear-
sing the word of God before the Lord—that we need to
learn—but to preach sermonettes or give Bible outlines is
preaching at God, and that is terrible.

The shopping list

Then there is what we call the 'shopping list' prayer or the
'world tour' prayer. Someone has probably had a great
battle in getting their mouth open, but finally they take the
plunge and then proceed to go through the lot, right down
the shopping list and all around the world, before they feel
they've done.

Artificiality

Another thing we have to avoid is sentiment and artifici-
ality. It was W.P. Nicholson who once said: 'Why do
people have to use strange voices when they speak to
God?' The 'prayer' is always and only used of speaking
with God. We must be reverent before the Lord, there
must be a fear of the Lord; but why do we have to be
artificial? We speak to the Lord in a way that we would
not dream of speaking to our husband or wife. Why is it
our Lord has to be treated to such an artificial way of
speaking? Why can't we speak with the Lord as we speak
with one another—only reverently?

Long prayers

When prayers go on too long it is usually repetition that is the problem.

Mechanical noise

What do I mean by this? I mean the noises that people make mechanically at certain points during prayers. Someone will say, 'Oh, Lord, Soviet Russia is so dark,' and there will be a grunt. Or think of the brother who has the idea that the word 'hallelujah!' is a kind of punctuation mark in his own or others' prayers.

It is a wonderful thing when someone really does say 'Hallelujah!', or when someone says 'Amen' or when someone says 'Yes, Lord!' out loud, when it really is from the Spirit. It is wonderful when a great chorus of 'Amens' goes up because we are all witnessing to that matter in the Spirit. But beware of becoming mechanical.

Praying into your hands

Speak up. Do not speak into your hands or into the chair. I have said it so many times and still people do it. They speak into their hands and you can't hear a word they are saying. They might as well be speaking in a tongue. It would be better, really, if they were. It is just like 1 Corinthians 14—we cannot say 'Amen' because we do not understand a word of what they say. If you have a soft voice, do not let that stop you from praying; but remember to speak out and keep it brief and to the point.

Insensitivity

Insensitivity to the leading of the Spirit of God, to the anointing, can be a real problem. Even if you are deaf and cannot always hear what is being said, you can still be in tune with the Spirit and follow his leading in the prayer time.

Sometimes insensitivity can take the form of slavishly going right through the whole list of prayer requests to the end. As soon as there is a moment of silence, we are on to the next point because we are not under the anointing. We are not being sensitive to the Spirit of God. Why should we have to pray for every item that is suggested? Maybe the Lord does not want to mention this or that. Some things will be prayed for at home. We need to be sensitive to the Spirit of God.

Awareness of God

What is our biggest problem? I have talked about the principle of prayer and four aspects of prayer and the right kind of prayer time and laid some practical points, but at the root of the whole matter is our need for an awareness of God.

Seventy-five per cent—if not eighty per cent, or more— of all our prayer is really for public consumption and not for divine attention; and the reason is, we are not aware of the Lord. Elijah referred three or four times to 'the Lord, before whom I stand'. No one could see him standing before the Lord. He may have been standing before King Ahab or Jezebel, but had such a consciousness, such an awareness of God, that he always said, 'The Lord, before whom I stand.'

Some people treat corporate prayer as a devotional exercise, others as some kind of duty that has got to be fulfilled—they feel they must pray for as much as possible in one go. All that would vanish if we were really aware of God. Even though we cannot see him with our physical eyes, God is actually in this place by his Spirit. If we were really aware of that, it would revolutionise our prayer. We would be so direct. We would say, 'Lord, you are here. You, the Master of the whole earth, are actually among us. We want to bring this need to you. We do not have to tell you everything. You know it all.'

A few words in the ear of the King of kings could change a situation. Some of us think, 'If only I had the influence, the power, I could change things.' But do you know that you can have an hour, again and again, in the presence of the King of kings? The tragedy is that, so often, that hour is lost in so much that is not real prayer. May the Lord graciously give to every one of us an awareness of his presence.

2

The Leading of the Spirit

And take the helmet of salvation, and the sword of the Spirit, which is the word of God: Praying always with all prayer and supplication in the Spirit, and watching thereunto with all perseverance and supplication for all saints (Ephesians 6:17–18).

But ye, beloved, building up yourselves on your most holy faith, praying in the Holy Ghost, Keep yourselves in the love of God, looking for the mercy of our Lord Jesus Christ unto eternal life (Jude 20–21).

Likewise the Spirit also helpeth our infirmities: for we know not what we should pray for as we ought: but the Spirit itself maketh intercession for us with groanings which cannot be uttered. And he that searcheth the hearts knoweth what is the mind of the Spirit, because he maketh intercession for the saints according to the will of God (Romans 8:26–27).

Behold, how good and how pleasant it is for brethren to dwell together in unity! It is like the precious ointment upon the head, that ran down upon the beard, even Aaron's beard: that went down to the skirts of his garments; As the dew of Hermon and as the dew that descended upon the mountains of Zion: for there the Lord commanded the blessing, even life for evermore (Psalm 133).

Without the Holy Spirit, there can be no real prayer. Without the Holy Spirit, a prayer meeting is a lot of human beings just simply giving voice to so many petitions. Real prayer is something which the Holy Spirit initiates, leads, directs and empowers in a very wonderful way. He brings us to the place where we execute the will of God. His leadership, direction, empowering and ministry are essential to corporate prayer. Without him, there can be no togetherness, no harmony, no anointing, and no weapons that are effectual.

When the Holy Spirit is quenched or grieved in a time of prayer, we simply become a congregation of units, quite unrelated, all doing our own thing. We may be biblical and quite correct, but we are simply a congregation of saved individuals who are totally unrelated. There can be no togetherness, no mutuality in expression. It is not that the anointing is not there for us, but that the anointing has not been recognised and has not been obeyed. If the Holy Spirit is not present, who can use the sword of the Spirit? It is impossible. The weapons of our warfare are not of the flesh; they do not belong to the realm of human genius or human resource or human energy. If the Holy Spirit is not present in his position as conductor and leader and director of the whole time of prayer, then there are no weapons. We may, quite correctly, try to stay focused, to a certain extent, on certain points. But we will never feel that anything has been dealt with, or that action has been taken by God. We may pray and pray, but things will not come to a conclusion because everything will still be in the realm of our own endeavour.

Who else but the Holy Spirit can make known to the members of Christ's body what is the will and the mind and the burden of the Head? How does the risen Christ in the midst of us make his mind known apart from the Spirit? We mentioned before those verses in Matthew

18: 'Again I say unto you, That if two of you shall agree on earth as touching any thing that they shall ask, it shall be done for them of my Father which is in heaven. For where two or three are gathered together in my name, there am I in the midst of them' (verses 19–20). How does the risen Christ bring about that inner agreement, that spontaneous organic oneness in the members of his body? It is only by the Holy Spirit. There is no other way.

That is why we are told in Ephesians 6:18 that we are to pray 'always with all prayer and supplication in the Spirit'. Now note very carefully this phrase *praying in the Spirit*. There is a common idea nowadays that to pray in the Spirit means to pray in a tongue. Now praying in the Spirit most definitely includes praying in a tongue. The gift of tongues, especially in devotion and in intercession, is a manifestation of the Spirit and is obviously praying in the Spirit. But to equate praying in the Spirit only with praying in a tongue is quite wrong and devalues the whole meaning of the phrase. Praying in the Spirit is a far greater thing than just praying in a tongue.

All real prayer is in the Spirit. It is under the leadership of the Spirit, under the direction of the Spirit, by the empowering of the Spirit. If we can get that clear, it will help us very much. The source of all true corporate prayer is in the Spirit. Now we can begin to recognise that corporate prayer is not just a 'get together' of human beings giving voice to their own burdens and petitions and feelings. We are now in another dimension. We are *in the Spirit*.

The absolute sovereignty of the Holy Spirit in prayer

The Holy Spirit is absolutely sovereign, and unless his sovereignty is recognised by everyone at the very commencement of a time of prayer, there will be a blockage to start with. A shadow will come into our

time of prayer. And it is not only just any Tom, Dick,
and Harry who can quench the Holy Spirit; sometimes
the leaders can do so.

A prayer time is not just a free-for-all where we can all
say our little bit. It is not a time for some sort of spiritual
self-expression, where you say your little piece and I say
my little piece, and we all express our spiritual character
and stature and standing together, and it helps us all. If we
view a prayer time like this there will be no question of us
getting anything done, no question of things in the heavenlies being touched, no question of principalities and
powers being set back.

The prayer time is not even just a time for the expression of petitions as *we* see the need. Just because you see a
need or feel a need does not necessarily mean that the
Lord himself wants that particular need brought into the
time of prayer.

Christ is the Head of the body. 'He has been made head
over all things to the church, which is his body, the fulness
of him that filleth all in all' (see Ephesians 1:22–23). What
does that mean? Why are we told over and over again, 'He
is head of the body;' 'He is the head of the church;' 'He is
head over all things to the church'? What does *head* mean,
if it does not represent the mind and the will? Surely, it
must speak of the mind of Christ and the will of Christ and
the design, in one sense, that is in his mind—his purpose
and his aim.

A head is not just empty, or is not meant to be. There is
intelligence in the head. A person's head is where he
thinks. The head is the place of the intelligence, the place
of will, the place of purpose. We cannot know the will of
our Head, except by the Holy Spirit. We cannot know the
design that he has except by the Holy Spirit. We cannot
know the aim that he has, except by the Holy Spirit. We
cannot know the burden that he has, except by the Holy

Spirit. Therefore, when we speak of the term 'head over all things to the church', we speak of his ascendancy. There is no other body in the world that the Lord Jesus has been made Head over, only the church. And we, as the body, need to acknowledge that lordship and that kingship, that ascendancy of the Lord Jesus Christ. We cannot do this except by the Holy Spirit.

You know as well as I do that a prayer time can be hard going and at the mercy of circumstances until and unless the Holy Spirit comes right into the situation. We may start off and find it really difficult. Then suddenly someone will pray under the anointing of the Holy Spirit and, in that moment, it is like a spiritual sound barrier has been broken and we are through onto a new level. The Holy Spirit is now in his rightful place. His sovereignty has been recognised, the anointing is being obeyed and in that moment, something happens.

Unless the Head can express his mind and his burden and his ascendancy and his victory, we can get nowhere. The Holy Spirit is sovereign, and he must be obeyed by every member. There is not a single one of us who is an exception to this rule. None of us is so mature in the Lord that we can be excused obedience to him. It is a serious thing to grieve the Holy Spirit.

Even worse, however, is the quenching of the Holy Spirit. Sometimes in a time of prayer, when everything is alive, someone will break in and cause the whole thing to nose-dive into death. What are we to do when this happens? Many people feel really embarrassed, but they do not want to cause a disturbance. They really want to be able to say 'Amen' to the prayer that has been prayed, but if they are faithful to the Lord, something inside them is saying, 'No Amen there. Don't be a partaker of that.' Never say 'Amen' just because you think that, in some sentimental way, you are helping someone. You will become a partaker of something that is not of God, and the Bible says you touch death. And one of the things a priest or a Levite must never do is touch death because, when you touch death, you become involved in death; you become compromised.

So we cannot be sentimental. Of course, we want to help one another, but when the prayer time takes a dive down into death, and we feel the Holy Spirit has been quenched, we need to be alive and sensitive to the Holy Spirit. It is possible to come back onto the track and for life to come straight in again. I am sure you have noticed that sometimes. Someone else comes in under the anointing and the whole place is full of 'Amens'. You cannot help it. It is because it is back under the anointing and the Spirit in you witnesses with your spirit: 'We are back on track.'

But it is a sad thing when we take a dive into death, and then someone else follows in death, and someone else follows in death; and the Holy Spirit is quenched and the time dies. We will go out more exhausted than we came in.

It is the Holy Spirit who makes known the mind of Christ, gives expression to his burden, directs us into the doing of his will, and establishes his victory. So it is vitally and strategically important that all of us recognise, obey, and begin to experience the Headship of Christ by the Spirit. Then the youngest believer will learn lessons that will stand him in good stead for the whole of his life down here and for his service in eternity. We will all learn to distinguish between soul and spirit. We will learn to distinguish the government of God. And we will learn as much from when things go wrong, as from when they go right.

In a time of prayer the Holy Spirit is like the conductor of an orchestra. All the members of the orchestra must keep their eyes on the conductor. It is no good just having your instrument to hand, and the music in front of you; you have got to have an eye on the conductor.

So often in a time of prayer people will have their instrument ready and both eyes firmly on the music, but then there comes a disharmony. Maybe the Lord wants you to contribute five times in one session of prayer. That is his business. If the baton points in your direction, in you come. If you were a violinist in an orchestra you wouldn't say, 'We have had our lot at the beginning and we are not coming in any more, no matter how much he points at us.' The triangle player doesn't bang it furiously all the way through a piece. The fact of the matter is we have got to be under the direction of the Conductor. The Holy Spirit is really 'symphonising' us; he is harmonising us; he is blending us together. If we will only keep our eyes on him, then every one of us has a part to play in the prayer time, and we shall be wholly with him and contributing what he has given us.

I believe that this can be so even when we do not actually contribute. I know that some people will hide behind that and say, 'Well, I am so glad he said that because I never take part, or very rarely, because I do not think the conductor ever points in my direction.' But maybe you're not looking. The Lord is a perfect gentleman, and if you say, 'I'm not taking part in this session, Lord,' he will ignore you. He will never draw you in unless you are willing. But there will come a day when you will stand before God and learn what you have lost. Unless we learn to overcome our reluctance—and that can be very hard sometimes—and contribute what we have of the Lord under the direction of the Spirit of God, then it seems to me that we shall not really be qualified for the eternal service for which God is wanting to train us.

When we all obey the Holy Spirit there will be a design, a harmony, a cohesion in the time, and a fulfilment in our prayer time. That is what it means to pray in the Spirit. It simply means we are under his direction. And because we are under his direction and leadership, and contributing by his prompting and enabling power, there will be harmony and cohesion and fulfilment in that whole time of prayer.

The purpose of the prayer time

In Matthew 6:10, Jesus teaches his disciples to pray, 'Thy kingdom come. Thy will be done, as in heaven, so on earth.' The purpose of corporate prayer is that together, as the people of God, we see that the will of God is done on earth as it is in heaven. First, we have to find out what the will of God is in heaven; and then we bring that will, as it is done in heaven, to earth. We cannot use the keys of the kingdom unless we know that heaven has first said 'yes'. Then we can use them. We are to see that the kingdom of God comes in the various situations we face.

Suppose a group of people who are involved in outreach and winning others to Christ should suddenly find that they are blockaded. What do they do? They may preach more and they find that they are just as blockaded. Or they may decide to change the whole time and have something altogether different, which may at least give everyone a jolt and shake them out of a rut. But very precious things can be lost that way because that is not the root of the problem. The root of the problem is that, somehow or other, we have got to get behind the scenes and see that the kingdom of God comes into this blockade.

Do you believe that Satan can ultimately blockade Christ? Do you think the gates of hell can prevail against the church—in flat contradiction to the words of our Lord Jesus in Matthew 16:18? Time and again I have seen that blockade building up and the people of God finding it harder and harder to break through. Now if we just pray, 'Oh Lord, please, please, please,' it just gets harder and harder and becomes heavier and heavier. But the moment we declare that Jesus Christ is Lord and assert that the kingdom of God has the final say in a situation, we see straight away that the grip of Satan has to loose on that whole matter. What is the kingdom of God? The kingdom of God is the throne of God. It is the kingship of the Lord Jesus. It is the rule of the Lord Jesus.

There can be all kinds of complex situations that we face: situations in a family, in an office, or locally in our life together as the people of God. Until we learn how to bring the kingdom of God into those situations, God will not bring the kingdom in. We must beware of the wrong kind of Calvinism which says that God will bring it in anyway. If you don't want the gates of hell to prevail against Christ's building of the church, then you must use the keys. If you want to see precious lives made living stones for that building work of the church, then you must use the keys. If you don't want the power of darkness and death to prevail against the church, then you must use the keys.

God is intent on teaching us lessons, like a father teaching a little child. If you do not learn while you are growing up, you will never learn. It is no good me or some other leader unlocking the kingdom of God for you all the time. You have got to learn to do it.

Watching and praying

Sometimes people learn to pray, but they do not watch. All the time things are happening—politically, economically, militarily, spiritually—on an international level, a national level and a local level. When something happens, we say, 'Look what has happened. Now we must pray.' Whereas, if we had been awake and watching, keeping alert and praying, we would have foreseen these events long before. Every single believer can be taught by the Spirit of God to spot things beforehand. The Spirit of God can teach even the biggest spiritual dimwit to spot things before they happen. What good are you going to be in the government and administration of God in eternity if you cannot spot things happening now? You may say to me, 'But there is no darkness, there are no problems in eternity.' I know there is no darkness (except a thing called outer darkness), but I am quite sure there will be problems of some kind. I think you will find that in eternity, life being life, there will be things, without sin, that we will have to untie. We are being trained for those situations, and only God can show us and teach us how to do it now.

The aim and purpose of our prayer times is that we should see fulfilled and realised the mind and will of our risen Head. In that time of prayer we are first to discover the mind of the Head and then to pour out our hearts in prayer and intercession and see that the mind of our Lord is realised in the situations that we are bringing to him. That aim should govern each step. Clearly, then, the time of prayer is not just for self-expression; it is not just a 'free-for-all'; but it is a time when we have got to keep alive and alert and obey the Lord.

The anointing for the prayer time

Everyone is clear on the need for an anointing when it comes to a preacher or a leader. People will travel miles and miles to hear an anointed preacher. Every believer knows very well that the preacher or the pastor or the evangelist or the teacher ought to have an anointing. And if he does not have it, we say something is wrong with him.

However, very few people ever see the need for an anointing for a meeting. It is an interesting thing that, in the Old Covenant, we find not only was the king anointed, not only was the priest anointed, not only was the prophet anointed, but all the furniture of the tabernacle was anointed and the tent of meeting was anointed (see Exodus 30:26). They anointed the tent of meeting where God met with the people and the people met with God. In other words, there is an anointing for our meetings with God and God's meetings with us. In Psalm 133 we read: 'Behold, how good and how pleasant it is for brethren to dwell together in unity!' This is not just about having a holiday together in unity, or a few days, or a few moments in unity, or a meeting, but we are to *dwell* together in unity.

'It is like the precious oil upon the head, that ran down upon the beard, even Aaron's beard; that came down upon the hem of his garment.' What is this all about? I remember when I first used to read that I would think, 'What an odd psalm—beards and heads and hems of garments and oil being poured.' Then it talks about the dew of Hermon coming down upon the mountains of Zion. What does the oil on Aaron's head and the picture of it coming down on his beard and onto his garments have to do with people being one? Aaron was the high priest and the oil is the Spirit of God. The only way our oneness can function in practical ways is by the anointing—the oil upon the head, running down upon the beard, right down to the hem of the garment. In other words, every single member of the body is included in the anointing.

That alone is sufficient for me to believe there is an

experience of the Holy Spirit that every one of us must
enter into. If we enter into it at our new birth, thank God—
although I find very few who do. We all need to enter into
an experience of the anointing. Of course, the Holy Spirit
is in us—no one is born of God without that—but we need
to know an anointing.

One of the titles of the Lord Jesus is 'Christ', which is
the Greek form of the Hebrew 'Messiah', 'the anointed
One'. In both Greek and Hebrew it means 'the anointed
One'. What does it mean to be 'in Christ'? It means that
you are in the anointed One. There is an anointing for you
in Christ. This is the meaning of Pentecost. The Head
received the promise of the Father and poured it out on
the body. The anointing came down upon 120 members,
and every one of them entered into their union with Christ
and into the anointing that was theirs. The Holy Spirit
came into them and upon them, and from that moment,
they knew an anointing. Every one of us has got an
anointing.

In the Old Testament anointing was God's sign: 'That
thing is set aside for my use.' There was to be no flesh.
That is why it says in Exodus 30:32 that the holy anointing
oil shall not touch the flesh. And if the flesh touched it,
that man would be stoned to death. It should never touch
the flesh nor should anyone make anything like it; it was
holy. It was because the holy anointing oil set a person
apart.

Now do you begin to understand why there is an
anointing for our meetings? The flesh ought not come
into our meetings. This is not the place for man's
ingenuity or creativity, for man's ability or resources,
for man's ideas or opinions—even if they are spiritual
opinions. The whole time should be set aside for the
Lord.

That is why the king was anointed. That is why the

prophet was anointed. That is why the priest was anointed. God was saying, 'That one is set aside from all that he is naturally for me. I will rule through him. I will pray through him. I will speak through him.'

When we see this, we can begin to understand the importance of this word 'anointing'. I know that I am always talking about the anointing, but I don't suppose too many really understand what I am talking about. 'There is an anointing,' I will often say. 'We stand into it for speaker and hearers alike.' Before coming to a time of prayer, I will often say, 'Lord, we stand into that anointing which is ours. We gather everybody into it.' Why do I do this? It is because I want to make sure that Satan knows very well that, as far as I am concerned, the prayer time is not going to be anything from my opinions or anyone else's opinions—it is for the Lord.

Nothing we do suffers more from our own opinions than the prayer time. No place is more at the mercy of our sentiments or our feelings. We must recognise that there is an anointing for every single time of prayer. If we were to meet seven times a week for prayer, there would be an anointing for all seven times—a fresh anointing every time. And the whole value of that time will depend upon whether we all—leaders and people alike—stand into the anointing from the beginning and right the way through.

The psalm says, 'For there the Lord commanded the blessing, even life for evermore.' And we have known that. When there is a time of prayer that is under the anointing, there is life. It floods through the whole time. It is just like the dew coming down from Hermon. The cold air of the north and the warm air of the south meet over the mountains of Zion and come down in dew. Because Jerusalem does not normally have rain for eight to nine months of the year, it relies on a heavy dew that comes every single night in the hottest part of the summer.

When we all stand in the anointing and recognise it in our time of prayer—or at any other time—and follow it, you know what happens? We will come in worn out and go out revived. The time can be a battle, but we will go out with a spring in our step. Sometimes, in our times of prayer, we may come in worn out and go out nearly dead. Senility overtakes us during the time. This is because there has not been an anointing obeyed by us all and, therefore, there is no dew and there is no life.

Few believers are able to recognise when that blessing of eternal life which God has commanded has been quenched. Many of us just go on with the routine—rather like the Laodiceans. They thought they had everything. They ambled on with all their meetings and their prayer meetings and their Bible studies and their evangelistic outreach, and they did not even know that the Lord was *outside* saying, 'Behold, I stand at the door and knock.' They must have thought this was scandalous: 'What kind of man is John that he can see such a thing—Jesus outside our group and asking to come in?'

We are always singing hymns to our Lord. We are always reading his word. We are always doing what we were taught to do twenty years ago, or a hundred years ago. But the fact of the matter is that there is an anointing, and it is necessary to abide under the anointing in our prayer times. That is how we can know when the prayer is alive or dead. Sometimes, a person's prayer is full of life, and then someone else comes in with a dead prayer. It is not that there is anything wrong with that person, it is just that they are not under the anointing; they are doing their own thing.

It is part of our spiritual education to learn to discern and to abide under the anointing. If the burden of the

Spirit and the mind of Christ for tonight is Nepal, it is no good praying for Laos. You may have had a letter hot from Laos, full of urgent needs, and you think, 'We must pray!' But the mind of the Lord may be, 'No—pray for Nepal.' When we obey the mind of the Lord—not our preconceived ideas, but the mind of the Lord—he will answer us because we have obeyed him. But the extraordinary thing is that he will answer Laos too because we obeyed him in praying for Nepal.

I remember in one of the schools of prayer, someone brought up the name of a dear sister who was very, very ill. We talked about her for twenty minutes or so at the beginning of the prayer time, and it was one of the worst times of prayer I have ever been in. The former sessions had been marvellous times, but on this occasion it took a dive, and there we all were, fumbling around. Information was given; there were sermonettes galore, horizontal prayers; stresses and strains coming out everywhere. The dear lady's name would go here, across, back, across, over here, and back again. Someone would come in with something else, and then back we would go to her.

And you know what? She was already dead! The brother who started the prayer was an old missionary who had heard that this lady was very ill. In actual fact, she had gone a day or two before. But he started off, and one or two others, who had kinks about healing, were absolutely sure that every believer ought to be healed—and said so. That is where the sermonettes came in. They were saying, 'You know, Lord, it says such and such in the Scriptures, and this person has *got* to be healed.'

We rumbled around in a mess and a confusion that was terribly hard to bear. I remember at the end of it one brother said, 'Oh Lord, we have fallen flat on our faces; help us,' and in fact the Lord turned that particular time of prayer into the most marvellous time of instruction for everybody. When we got back on track it was tremendous; it went like a bomb.

If God says, 'Pray for this,' don't pray for something else. Don't say, 'But if we don't pray for so and so, they will die.' The Lord says, 'You leave that to me. You do what I am telling you to do, not what you think is right to do. If I tell you to pray for Japan, brother so and so is going to get healed along the way because you are obeying me in faith.'

In our unbelief we so often feel that unless we open our big mouth and say something it will not get done. Therefore, we pray for what God has not directed us to pray for, we are not under the anointing, and we get into death. Then we don't pray for the thing God wants, and the thing that we want to see happen cannot happen anyway because we have not been under the anointing. So we are in a complete mess.

So you can see that this whole matter of the anointing is not only a matter of divine government, it is a matter of divine discipline. We have to be disciplined by one another; we have to be disciplined by the Spirit of God. And we can only learn as we are prepared to make mistakes. Every one of us has made mistakes in the place of prayer, but as long as we learn from those mistakes, all is well. That is part of our discipline. It is when we make the same mistake again and again that there is something terribly and radically wrong.

Practical points

First, we must look to the Spirit to lead us not only at the beginning of the prayer time, but throughout.

Secondly, the person with responsibility for leadership should always assert the headship of Christ over the time before beginning. Never go into a time of prayer without two or three of you coming before the Lord and declaring that Jesus Christ is Lord of this time and Head over all things.

Thirdly, we must learn to know when to pray and—just as importantly—when to stop praying. It is not always easy when, after a great battle, you finally open your mouth and are in full flood. But it is a sad thing when people can't stop and can't distinguish when the anointing has gone from them.

Fourthly, we must learn to assess when a matter is settled and also when the Lord has moved on to something else. Not every single matter raised in a prayer time has got to be settled in that time—that would be a legalistic attitude. It is not easy to be led by the Spirit, but there are times when the Lord brings up a matter and seven, ten, twelve people may pray for it from different angles; and then the Lord says, 'That is enough for this evening. We shall take this matter up again.'

There are some people whose idea of prayer is to walk around Jericho until the walls drop. But it will not be the walls that drop. Don't wear yourself out in matters of prayer that are not under divine direction. Listen carefully to what the Lord says. He said to Joshua and the people of Israel, 'Once around for six days, and on the seventh day, seven times around.' It would have done them no good on that first day to continue to walk around for twenty-four hours. They would have been finished—with blisters and terrible foot sores—and still would not have seen the walls come down.

Learn to assess when a matter is settled and be ready to introduce a new matter under the government of the Spirit. Be careful of a slavish, mechanical following of an agenda for prayer. Be alive and sensitive to the Spirit.

Fifthly, we must learn how to respond when something

not under the anointing is introduced. When someone begins praying and the prayer does not feel right or it is misplaced or a sermonette or a horizontal prayer or information giving, don't be tempted to think that is the end and you just give up. That is not the end at all. Maybe the Lord will teach you through such mistakes. Sometimes our prayer times do seem to go in and out—one moment we are on track, the next we go astray. But the Lord may say that was a good time of prayer because, basically, we kept on track, and in the end of it we went out under the anointing. But where we go wrong is when we go off at a tangent. Then indeed the whole thing is finished, and the Lord will leave our prayer time saying, 'Carry on. You appear to feel that you can do it better without my help or direction, so carry on.'

Sixthly, be careful not to let sentiment govern your sense of priorities. Emergencies may appear that seem to require immediate attention. If the Lord directs that we should take them up, then we must do so. But there are times when the Lord does not, and we need to listen only to him.

Seventhly, those with responsibility for leadership must listen carefully to the suggested matters for prayer. Remember they are only *suggested* matters. It is up to us to look to the Lord to see what he wants us to concentrate on, or if there is something else entirely that should be included.

Eighthly, those with responsibility for leadership should be alive to the need on occasion to correct. When there are people who are failing again and again, then I think there is the need for a word of correction. Alternatively, when someone really is a means of bringing life into a time of prayer, that person should be encouraged. So often, the person who is alive and under the anointing is the one who gets discouraged, and the person making mistakes goes on like a tank.

Lastly, remember that *all* of us are disciples. We are *all* learning in 'the school of prayer'.

3

Watching and Praying

Watch and pray, that ye enter not into temptation: the spirit indeed is willing, but the flesh is weak (Matthew 26:41).

One wonders what would have happened if those disciples had only been alive enough, when our Lord said that word, to obey it. Their moment of temptation was about to come and they did not know it; and even when the Lord spoke to them, they were not really aware of their need. So when they entered into the severest test that any of them had faced, every one of them failed. And our Lord had said to them, 'Watch and pray, that ye enter not into temptation.'

He understood their condition. It was not as if he was condemning them and saying, 'Oh dear, you are all so bound by your flesh.' He understood their frame and their physical make-up and their mental make-up. He understood everything about them; and so he gave this word.

I do not suppose a single one of us would know times of defeat if we could only learn to watch and pray. So often we wait until we are in the midst of the trial to pray. We wait until we are right in the heart of the conflict, when everything is dark and devilish and complex and it seems as if we are cut off from the Lord, and then we start to pray. If only we would 'watch and pray'.

> Take ye heed, watch and pray: for ye know not when the time
> is. For the Son of man is as a man taking a far journey, who
> left his house, and gave authority to his servants, and to every
> man his work, and commanded the porter to watch. Watch ye
> therefore: for ye know not when the master of the house
> cometh, at even, or at midnight, or at the cockcrowing, or
> in the morning: Lest coming suddenly he find you sleeping.
> And what I say unto you I say unto all, Watch (Mark 13:33–
> 37).

What does Jesus mean, 'Watch and pray for ye know not
when the time is'? He obviously did not mean that by
watching and praying we would know *when* he was about
to return, for we know that no one knows that day or hour.
I believe he means that by watching and praying we will
see the movements in the unseen. It is not that we have got
to know when the Lord is coming; our great need is to be
alive to Satan's devices, so that when the enemy seeks to
undo us or trap us or compromise us or put us into a place
of pressure, we will be alive to it.

Personally I have no doubt that when the days come
which are spoken of in Revelation 13—the mark of the
beast, 666, and all that—there will be so many pressures
that most of the people of God, apart from the grace of
God, will compromise. We have seen it in the past:
confusion, perplexity, darkness, weakness among the
people of God. There has been no clear voice, no clear
understanding of the issues involved. We all get frightened and run to extremes. And so it will always be unless
we watch and pray.

> Then shall two be in the field; the one shall be taken, and the
> other left. Two women shall be grinding at the mill; the one
> shall be taken, and the other left. Watch therefore: for ye
> know not what hour your Lord doth come (Matthew 24:40–
> 42).

Don't let the enemy get you into such a position that you are compromised or defeated or living in sin.

> And take heed to yourselves, lest at any time your hearts be overcharged with surfeiting, and drunkenness, and cares of this life, and so that day come upon you unawares. For as a snare shall it come on all them that dwell on the face of the whole earth. Watch ye therefore, and pray always, that ye may be accounted worthy to escape all these things that shall come to pass, and to stand before the Son of man (Luke 21:34–36).

Most people would feel that surfeiting is wrong, and undoubtedly all would think that drunkenness is wrong. But 'the cares of this life' affect every single one of us. And maybe it will not be surfeiting or drunkenness that will undo many a child of God but the cares of this life; just the routine of life. That is what I find most sad about the people of God. We are all the same. We get into a routine and round we go in the routine. As it gets busier, and there are more and more pressures on us and more and more calls on our time, we just go round and round; and we do not watch. We are caught up in the machinery that is going on and on. 'Watch ye therefore, and pray always, that ye may be accounted worthy to escape all these things that shall come to pass.'

> And take the helmet of salvation, and the sword of the Spirit, which is the word of God: Praying always with all prayer and supplication in the Spirit, and watching thereunto with all perseverance and supplication for all saints (Ephesians 6:17–18).

In this matter of watching, we really need perseverance. So often, when we use the word 'watch', people think of 'watch night services' or 'watchman on the walls' or that kind of thing—all of which is right. But if you just remember that a watchman is someone who keeps awake while everybody else sleeps, you will get nearer to an understanding of what it is to watch. The Greek word just means 'keep awake'. If you think of it like that, it is so clear. Keep awake! Keep alert! Keep alive! You cannot watch if you are drowsy or half asleep. You will not notice anything. So the word is: watching thereunto with all perseverance. This is a matter where we have got to take ourselves to task.

And it is not enough just to stay awake. There are times when we will feel like sleeping, and we are going to have to take some strong spiritual black coffee to keep us awake and keep us alert and alive. We will not be able just to rely on our natural resources and natural energy. We shall need something more than that.

> Continue in prayer, and watch in the same with thanksgiving;
> Withal praying also for us (Colossians 4:2–3a).

Now some people's idea of keeping awake is that the whole thing is a grim, dour business and the grimmer you are, the more awake you are. They think we have to be so solemn about this matter of keeping awake, of watching—so intense. But Paul says here that we are to watch 'with thanksgiving'. Let there be a bit of joy in this keeping awake. Actually, being joyful will probably keep you awake better than anything else. When you have a bit of joy, you do not feel like going to sleep.

We are not to let this just be a kind of grim ministry focused upon the powers of darkness, looking all the time at the powers of evil and darkness and the way they are insidiously working—their devices, their authority, and all the rest of it. We won't find much cause for thanksgiving there. No, we are to give thanksgiving for our Lord—for his power, for his throne, for his mercy, for his grace, for what he is.

I feel that many times our prayer ministry deteriorates

into just prayer. It just becomes routine because we are not alive, we are not alert and watching what is happening. We are not keeping awake. We do not see the shifting scenes in the heavenlies or the movements of principalities and powers and world-rulers of this darkness. God does not want to be carrying us like babies all the time. He wants us to use the spiritual eyes he has given us.

> Watch ye, stand fast in the faith, quit you like men, be strong. Let all your things be done with charity (1 Corinthians 16:13–14).

The apostle Paul ends another of his letters by again saying, 'Watch.' This is not some subsidiary thing. It is vital that we keep alive and keep awake. If someone is going downhill we need to be aware before the collapse comes. We need to watch in the small matters of life, as well as in the big situations. If we let go, we will have lost something very precious, and the enemy will know it.

> Be sober, be vigilant; because your adversary the devil, as a roaring lion, walketh about, seeking whom he may devour: Whom resist stedfast in the faith, knowing that the same afflictions are accomplished in your brethren that are in the world (1 Peter 5:8–9).

It is no good just being sober. Some Christians are certainly sober, but they are not watchful. I know many sober Christians who are getting just as compromised by the enemy as some of the others. Oh, yes, they are sound; and they dot their 'i's' and cross their 't's', but they are not alive; they are not awake. Therefore, they can be easily trapped by the enemy.

Have you really understood that the devil is a roaring lion? I remember years ago, a couple of us took our Sunday school class to the zoo. Most of the children were just dreadful. They were all over the place, and I had visions of hands vanishing into tigers' stomachs. I decided the best thing to do was to stand with my back to the cage and watch them. Just at that moment the lion in the cage behind me roared. I don't know if it was hungry or calling to its mate or what, but to the delight of all the children I nearly collapsed into a heap.

The Scripture tells us that the devil is walking around as a roaring lion. Sometimes his very roar makes us almost feel that we have been eaten. But his roar is nothing. His bark is worse than his bite, and that is why we must withstand him. Don't worry about the roars of the devil—you are as safe as you can be if only you will be sober and watchful. Keep alive! Keep awake! Or you may find yourself in the stomach of the roaring lion.

> But ye, brethren, are not in darkness, that that day should overtake you as a thief. Ye are all the children of light, and the children of the day: we are not of the night, nor of darkness. Therefore let us not sleep, as do others; but let us watch [or keep awake] and be sober. For they that sleep sleep in the night; and they that be drunken are drunken in the night. [Watching overcomes sleep and being sober overcomes drunkenness.] But let us, who are of the day, be sober, putting on the breastplate of faith and love; and for an helmet, the hope of salvation. For God hath not appointed us to wrath, but to obtain salvation by our Lord Jesus Christ (1 Thessalonians 5:4–9).

> Be watchful, and strengthen the things which remain, that are ready to die: for I have not found thy works perfect before God (Revelation 3:2).

Some translations render this verse 'I have not found any of your works perfected.' Nothing has been completed. You started well, but nothing has been completed. Are there not a lot of us like that? We are always starting things which we never finish. We start courses which we never finish. We prepare for exams which we never go through with. It is something to beware of, for the Lord says to his church, 'Watch and establish those things that remain, for I have found nothing completed.'

> Behold, I come as a thief. Blessed is he that watcheth, and keepeth his garments, lest he walk naked, and they see his shame (Revelation 16:15).

How easy it is to steal from someone who is asleep. In other words, if you do not keep alive and awake, you may lose a lot. The enemy will see to that.

> Therefore watch, and remember, that by the space of three years I ceased not to warn every one night and day with tears (Acts 20:31).

Summary

First, we need to keep awake; and this watchfulness is related to prayer. We may see the necessity for prayer, but we must not allow the enemy to allow us to forget to combine that with watching. The two things go together. Any prayer ministry that does not keep awake and alert will, in the end, become just an empty routine.

Secondly, the reason we so often enter trials and tests is because we do not watch and pray. There are things happening in our nation; there are things happening locally; there are things happening among us as the people of God which we need to be alive and awake to, so that we can take action in time.

At one time there was an organisation which planned to open a sex shop in the town where I lived. As a church we were aware that such shops were becoming a problem all over the country and we were keeping alive and awake to the whole situation. On the day that the shop opened one of our members noticed it and came in and told us. We had

a time of prayer that evening, and what a time of prayer
we had! Now some people might ask why we should
worry about something like this. Surely, they say, the
world is going to pieces. The Bible says it's going to
get worse and worse and worse. Isn't it better just to
leave them to get on with it?

But we didn't think like that. We prayed, and we had a
wonderful time of prayer where many people stamped all
over that porn shop by faith—destroying it, liquidating it,
smashing it up. I really got carried away, and summed it
all up by saying, 'Oh Lord, put a bomb under that shop
and blow it up!'

The next morning one of the ladies in the church came
in laughing so much that, for a long time, she could not
tell us what was so funny. Finally, she got it out: 'The
porn shop! It's been blown up!' Then it was my turn to
have kittens. I thought the police would be round right
away. They knew we had written letters objecting to the
shop, but they had told us they could do nothing. I
imagined them confronting me: 'Mr Lambert, do you
have any reason to suspect any member of your congregation could have possibly put a bomb under this shop?'

I would say, 'Of course not.' But supposing one of the
more naïve among us should reply, 'No, but our minister
did pray that the Lord would put a bomb under it!'? I had
visions of trying to explain to some magistrate.

Apparently the gas heater had overheated and blown up
and the explosion had wrecked the place. The organisation
was not insured—they had been going to sign the insur-
ance the next day—so they lost everything. The place
closed down and, thank God, we never had that sex shop.

Because we were watchful on this issue, and acted
before it had gone too far, the Lord could come right in
and deal with it. He wants to do this in all kinds of
national, international, and church situations—if we will

stay awake. Most of the time we just jog along and don't really know what is happening until it is too late to do anything.

God told Jonah to go to Nineveh because he was going to destroy that city. And Jonah went and gave his message after quite a roundabout trip—by way of the big fish's stomach and a few other related lessons. But he finally got to Nineveh where he delivered the message of judgement with all the gusto that was in him. He rather enjoyed it because he had no particular love for the peole of Nineveh or the Assyrians. When the whole place repented, God deferred judgement for a whole generation. The judgement did finally come and Ninevch was wiped from the face of the earth, but God deferred it for a whole generation. God is not a machine. He responds to intercession, and he responds to repentance on the part of those who would be judged. We need to watch and pray in international and national situations.

We need to watch and pray in local church situations. We need to see the people of God brought together. There are many ways in which the enemy is seeking to come in and divide the people of God again. How we need to be alive and awake!

Parents need to watch and pray. Some parents' idea seems to be that the state cares for their children materially, the school cares for their children educationally, and the church cares for their children spiritually. All they do is live with them. Then they wonder why their children do not come to the Lord. I have noticed that where God has really started to save families, it has often been that someone in that family has got up early to pray. They have not been heavy-handed, all the time pushing the gospel; but they have watched, they have been awake, and they have prayed. I think that is the kind of concern that God takes note of. After all, parents, your prime responsibility, in the Lord, is your children.

So, on every level, we need to watch and pray that God, by his grace and in his mercy, may keep us awake and alive until his coming.

4

The Manifestation of the Spirit

Now there are varieties of gifts, but the same Spirit. And there are varieties of ministries, and the same Lord. And there are varieties of effects, but the same God who works all things in all persons. But to each one is given the manifestation of the Spirit for the common good. For to one is given the word of wisdom through the Spirit, and to another the word of knowledge according to the same Spirit; to another faith by the same Spirit, and to another gifts of healing by the one Spirit, and to another the effecting of miracles, and to another prophecy, and to another the distinguishing of spirits, to another various kinds of tongues, and to another the interpretation of tongues. But one and the same Spirit works all these things, distributing to each one individually just as He wills. For even as the body is one and yet has many members, and all the members of the body, though they are many, are one body, so also is Christ. For by one Spirit we were all baptized into one body, whether Jews or Greeks, whether slaves or free, and we were all made to drink of one Spirit. For the body is not one member, but many. If the foot should say, 'Because I am not a hand, I am not a part of the body,' it is not for this reason any the less a part of the body. And if the ear should say, 'Because I am not an eye, I am not a part of the body,' it is not for this reason any the less a part of the body. If the whole body were an eye, where would the hearing be? If the whole were hearing, where would the sense of smell be? But now God has placed the members, each one of them, in the body, just as He desired. And if they were all one member, where would the body be? But now there are many members, but one body (1 Corinthians 12:4–20, NASB).

And take the helmet of salvation, and the sword of the Spirit, which is the word of God: Praying always with all prayer and supplication in the Spirit, and watching thereunto with all perseverance and supplication for all saints (Ephesians 6:17–18).

Likewise the Spirit also helpeth our infirmities: for we know not what we should pray for as we ought: but the Spirit itself maketh intercession for us with groanings which cannot be uttered. And he that searcheth the hearts knoweth what is the mind of the Spirit, because he maketh intercession for the saints according to the will of God (Romans 8:26–27).

In one sense, all true prayer is a manifestation of the Spirit. This is something very wonderful because in many ways the deepest mystery about prayer is that what comes out in audible, understandable words is like the tip of an iceberg; the majority is hidden and inaudible. This is the ministry of the Holy Spirit in the believers.

This is not just for the great saints. It is for 'all the saints'. How wonderful that there is in us this ministry of the Holy Spirit—deeper than utterance, deeper than words, deeper than even a tongue. It is something that cannot get out in any kind of audible language but is the intercession of the Holy Spirit in us and it is according to the will of God. So genuine prayer is, in that sense, always a manifestation of the Holy Spirit. Most of it is buried deep within our spirit, and that which comes out in words is the manifestation, the uncovering of the mind of the Holy Spirit as he enables us in our poor words to pour out our soul to God.

All true prayer is in the Spirit. We have seen that praying in the Spirit is not just speaking in tongues, as some would have us understand. It includes that, but it is far, far greater than that. It is a dimension into which we enter when we pray. We pray in the Spirit. It is his burden that gives rise to our prayer. He conceives the prayer, he prompts, he leads, he enables us to pray. We are in and under the anointing. He is the One who harmonises us together. Corporate prayer takes place in the realm and dimension of the Spirit.

The Spirit manifests himself in corporate prayer

Now if this is true, then prayer in the Spirit must include the manifestation of the Spirit. If we are going to 'pray at all seasons in the Spirit', there must be times when the Holy Spirit will manifest himself in our times of prayer in specific ways; not just in the general sense that all prayer is a manifestation of the Spirit, but in specific ways.

In 1 Corinthians 12:7 we read that 'to each one is given the manifestation of the Spirit for the common good' (NASB).

It is to uncover and reveal

The word 'manifestation' literally means 'to make visible, to make clear, to make known'. Essentially it has this idea of uncovering, of laying bare, or revealing. When we understand that, we see what this manifestation of the Spirit is all about. It is the Holy Spirit uncovering the mind of Christ, uncovering the will of Christ, uncovering, as it were, the burden of Christ. Sometimes, in prayer, we dimly understand what the mind of the Lord is on a matter, but it is not clear. Now the manifestation of the Spirit can give a crystal clarity to our time of prayer by pinpointing something which makes every member of the body say,

'This is it!' So the manifestation of the Spirit makes a matter clear.

Sometimes we just need to know something. We are not quite sure what we are up against. We may feel all kinds of things in the atmosphere, but we do not know what they are. And the enemy may whisper in our ear all kinds of suggestions as to what is happening which may have nothing to do with it at all. So we end up with lots of cross-currents going backwards and forwards which destroy any possibility of the Holy Spirit harmonising us.

It is a wonderful thing when there can be a manifestation of the Spirit by which can come a revelation of the mind of the Lord. If the Lord Jesus has been made Head over all things to the church, then it seems to me logical to expect that he will in some way make known to us, in practical terms, how we are to pray or what we are to pray for.

There are times, of course, when we do not need any special manifestation of the Spirit, where it is absolutely clear to all of us. But there are other times when we are not clear and we need to have that manifestation, that uncovering, that laying bare of the heart of God by the Spirit of God.

It is for profit

I want you also to note that little phrase 'to profit'. The King James Version of 1 Corinthians 12:7 says, 'But the manifestation of the Spirit is given to every man to profit withal.' It is to our advantage. The New American Standard puts it very lucidly: 'for the common good'. It seems that if we are really all going to be in on this thing and all clear and all together and all harmonised, there are times when the Holy Spirit will manifest himself in some way and thus clarify things. And what is it all for? It is for the common good so that we are all together in this matter; we are all in on the good of it; it is for the profit of the whole body.

It is to each one

The whole context of this verse is the body of Christ—to each member of the body of Christ is the manifestation of the Spirit given for the common good.

Now we have already seen that the principle of corporate prayer is mutuality or togetherness. In other words, we have seen that the principle of corporate prayer is that we are one body in Christ. We belong to one another. Not one single one of us has it all. We belong to him and to one another. We are not one body of Christ, but one body in Christ; that is a little more (see Romans 12:5).

How can we know in practical experience in times of corporate prayer that we are one body in Christ? Our risen Head wants to transmit his mind; he wants to make known his will; he wants to act through us in the place of prayer. This means that every single one of us must be available to the Holy Spirit's ministry so that he can manifest himself in any way he wills in any time of prayer.

'Again I say unto you, That if two of you shall agree on earth as touching any thing that they shall ask, it shall be done for them of my Father which is in heaven. For where two or three are gathered together in my name, there am I in the midst of them' (Matthew 18:19–20). Here we have this whole thought of being in the body. We talked about being gathered into the name of the Lord and what it really means to be in the body of Christ, to be in him.

'Put on the whole armour of God, that ye may be able to stand against the wiles of the devil. Wherefore take unto you the whole armour of God, that ye may be able to withstand in the evil day, and having done all, to stand.

Stand therefore, having your loins girt about with truth
. . .' (Ephesians 6:11, 13–14a).

Some people get into a neurotic state over this armour
business. They remember to put on the helmet of salvation; and then they remember to put something on their
feet, the preparation of the gospel of peace; and they
forget their loins. Or they get the breastplate on and
they forget the shield. And some people, even when
they have put the whole lot on, feel that some way or
other they have missed a piece so they could not possibly
go out. In actual fact, this armour of God is the Lord Jesus
himself. Who is truth? He is truth. It is his faith, the faith
which is in the Son of God. The helmet of salvation—the
Lord Jesus is our salvation. The feet shod with the preparation of the gospel of peace—it is his gospel, and he is
our peace. Every part is there. The apostle puts it in
another letter: 'Put ye on the Lord Jesus Christ, and
make not provision for the flesh, to fulfil the lusts
thereof' (Romans 13:14). This is just putting it another
way: 'Put ye on the Lord Jesus Christ.' That is the whole
armour of God.

The command in Ephesians 6 is in the plural; it is to all
of us as members of Christ's body. We are to put on the
whole armour. We are to take our position in Christ. And
then, when we have taken our position in Christ, we are to
'take the sword of the Spirit, which is the word of God:
praying always with all prayer and supplication in the
Spirit, and watching thereunto with all perseverance and
supplication for all the saints'.

This togetherness in prayer, this mutuality, this being
agreed so that the matter is settled in heaven by our Father
can only be experienced as we pray in the Spirit. It is
precisely in this connection that the Holy Spirit manifests
himself as he wills through different members of the body.
There are times when we need to know what the enemy is

doing and what the aim of the enemy is. There are times when we need to know what is behind a particular problem. Otherwise, we can beat around the bush for not only hours but weeks and the thing is never touched because the finger of God has not been placed upon the facts of the matter and we are therefore unable to deal with it.

It is given

There are people who have permanent gifts, and those people are given as gifts to the church. For instance, there is the prophet. This is someone who has the gift of prophecy, but he or she is a prophet or prophetess as a gift. There may be someone who has a particular gift in interpreting tongues, and that may be something that is a permanent gift in them. However, we must also understand that the manifestation of the Spirit is not just permanently located in particular members of the body, but can be given wherever he wills. In other words, the Holy Spirit, at any given moment, can speak through a person who has never prophesied before; or a word of knowledge may be given to another who has never had such a thing before. There are some people who have the gift of faith. Hudson Taylor had the gift of faith; George Müller had the gift of faith; Gladys Aylward had the gift of faith; and there are others today who have the gift of faith. It is permanently located in them. They are gifts to the body of Christ, and their gift is to be those who exercise faith. But have you not had the experience in a time of prayer when suddenly you know in your heart that something had been done? The Holy Spirit manifested himself in you as faith. The gift of faith was manifested and you knew it. Your gift to the church is not that you are one who has been given the gift of faith in a peculiar way, but there are times when it is manifested in you.

It is wonderful when the Holy Spirit manifests himself through the body. At any given moment he can do as he wills. He may give the gift of healing; and someone who has never had it before knows in their heart that they can go and pray for someone and that person will be touched and healed, because of the gift of the Lord.

So we see that the Holy Spirit can manifest himself at any given moment. This is something very thrilling and exciting and can transform our gatherings. Thank God that we have permanent gifts among us, but how wonderful that we don't have to sit there in a kind of dullness waiting for brother so and so to perform. We can all look to the Holy Spirit at any moment for him to use us 'just as he wills'.

It is for the building up of the body

We need to understand that the Holy Spirit may manifest the gift of prophecy, or a word of knowledge, or faith in any member of the body of Christ as he sees fit, and for the common good. In this way, the whole body is saved from schism in the sense that we all belong to each other. From my point of view, it would be wonderful if only I had certain gifts, and you were all utterly dependent upon me for those. But when it comes to the building of the house of God, from without to within, I have certain gifts, others have certain gifts. We may have been given prophetic gifts; we may have been given evangelistic gifts, teaching gifts, other kinds of gifts, but they have been given to us for the building of the house. The body builds itself up in love, and this kind of manifestation of the Holy Spirit is for the building up of the body itself.

Suppose the Communists, or some other Fascist type of system, took over our country and swept away all the prophets, pastors, teachers, evangelists, healers, all the workers of miracles, everyone in any kind of responsible position and put them all in jail, and then martyred the lot. Are you going to tell me that would be the end of the church? I hope not!

If only we could learn that if we were all to look to the Lord and be available to the Holy Spirit, then at any given moment he could manifest himself—here in prophecy, there in a word of knowledge, here in wisdom, there in faith—then maybe we could do away with our one-man-band complex. This applies also to the contributing of a hymn, a part of the word, a word of revelation, or whatever the Spirit directs.

The direction of the Spirit

You all know the kind of prayer meeting where there is no direction. We drift. And what happens when we drift? We all fall back on routine. We just go on doing what we feel might at least do some good somewhere. And then before we know where we are, we have the sermonettes, the information giving, the precis of various parts of the word, and all the other things that come in because we are drifting. We have no clear direction on the matter. But when the Holy Spirit gives direction, then the whole time is transformed into a powerhouse.

How can he direct us when we want to know what the will of the Lord is on a particular matter? Sometimes, the Holy Spirit manifests himself in such a way that it becomes clear what is his will. It is not that someone gives us their opinion, but in different ways, somehow or other, someone communicates something from the Lord that is clear. It may come through the reading of a scripture. There is a burning in someone's heart, and the scripture they bring becomes a word of prophecy. The direction of the Spirit of God has come into that time of prayer.

Now I have known it happen that a scripture is given in this way and not a soul has taken it up because, for some reason, most people are half asleep. It is only human that sometimes we rest a little, or doze through a time of prayer. I think people sometimes do actually doze off, because when they wake up and join in, their prayers have no relationship whatsoever to anything that has gone before. We are to be awake and watchful and if the Lord has said something, then it is incumbent upon every member of the body to take it up. If we do not, we lose everything.

Now the Lord understands our failings, but it is better not to pray for a matter than to raise a matter and not carry it through to conclusion. Every time you touch the enemy on a sore spot, he does not forget. That is why it is tremendously important when we raise a matter, to take it through and not just let it go. Otherwise, those clouds of heaviness and death we sometimes feel are a direct result of the fact that we have raised a matter and left it in weakness. Then the enemy takes advantage and we can't understand why.

Sometimes we just need to establish the facts. We may have a problem before us for prayer. We are going to pray. Maybe it is a particular person; maybe it is a person's circumstances; maybe it is some situation abroad. Here is a real problem. It is all very well to say in a general way, 'Lord, give them wisdom,' but perhaps the Lord wants to give us the facts. Now he does not always do this; but there are times when we need to know the facts. This is where we need a word of knowledge—and the Holy Spirit can transmit it.

He is the supreme intelligence; he knows everything that is happening at once all through the world. We can't take in everything that is happening all at once, in thousands of individual lives, in different localities, in different groups of the Lord's people, but he knows every single thing; and there is not a single life that is not open before him. People talk about psychiatrists, but the Holy Spirit can see through every person. He knows what makes them tick; he knows their kind of mind, their background, what their motivating force is, the factors that lie behind it; he knows it all. So when a company of people start to pray, the Holy Spirit can start to transmit that knowledge.

It may not always be in a way that is clear, in the sense that there is a word of knowledge or a word of wisdom. A group may be praying for someone whom none of them knows. They may live thousands of miles away from the person they are praying for. And yet again and again in situations like these I have heard people prayed for as if some of those praying had known that person all their life. People start to pray and one layer comes off. Then someone else says, 'Lord, I feel that *this* is the thing.' That gets taken up by three or four people and they strip off another layer. Before long, they are down to the root of the problem. Now who else could have transmitted to those people what were the facts about that life but the Spirit of God? Who else knew the person?

There are times when we need to know the facts, and that is a word of knowledge. There are times when we need to know what to do with the facts. It is all very well to know the facts, but they can sometimes be very depressing. The fact is, sometimes we need to have a word of wisdom; we need to know what our response should be to these facts and what action we should take in prayer.

Some of us tend to use a sledge hammer in prayer. Our way of attacking everything is simply to batter the thing to death. But there are times when the Lord would take a knife and simply cut out one affected area, and with one or two strokes just get rid of the whole thing. This is another manifestation of the Spirit.

Suppose we are praying for a spiritual problem, for instance, someone who is totally blind and bound and oppressed by the devil. For some reason, whatever spirit it is will not release its hold of that life until the spirit is identified; but once it is identified, it will go. That is where we need to have the discerning of spirits to know what is behind the situation. And it is not only people who are demon possessed who are in need of this. Sometimes a situation exists because there is a spirit, a particular kind of spirit, that is sitting on the whole thing. And you can pray and pray and pray; but until you have got that revelation, the situation is not touched.

Sometimes, we need faith to take a position or maintain it. We may have prayed about a certain matter for a while but we need faith to cut through everyone's unbelief. Sometimes, a person has faith, and they may actually pray thanking the Lord for it. Then if we are all alive to it we will rise up and say, 'Yes, that is right!' We know in our hearts that the Holy Spirit has manifested himself in that person's faith, and now we all have a witness in our hearts that it is right. Sometimes, we have to maintain a position. Having taken a position, we lose it because there is not the faith.

Sometimes, we need a word of correction, or a word of encouragement, or a word of comfort. How sad when that doesn't come. We do not need it all the time, but I am sure there have been times for all of us when such a word from the Lord was needed to lift us all up and strengthen us. So often in the warfare of prayer, our hearts and spirits become weighed down by enemy pressure or become confused and weakened by his tactics and devices. It is precisely then that we need to know the manifestation of the Spirit. We need to know the facts about such heaviness. We need to know it is the enemy. Then we will know what to do.

Sometimes, we just need to praise the Lord. Many of you, I know, have found that one way is not to think about the enemy, but just praise the Lord—and that finishes him and the whole situation is broken open. At other times we have to declare the facts about the situation—that is, from God's point of view—and the enemy will be finished. There are other times when we need to be still. I have not seen that often because people seem to find it very hard to hear the word of the Lord in this way. But occasionally the way through a situation is just simply to do nothing and to be still. That is the greatest expression of faith there can be.

This is what is meant by the manifestation of the Spirit. Our risen Head knows exactly what we need to do and how we should do it; and by the manifestation of the Spirit, he directs us.

The gifts of the Spirit

The gifts of the Spirit are the equipment, the tools or the weapons with which we can do the job the Lord wants us to do. And while those gifts apply to much more than just corporate prayer, they are strategic and vital if we are to be directed accurately and efficiently. Now I sometimes think that if we knew a little more of this, some of our times of prayer could be cut down considerably. We would not need to go round and round the matter because the Lord could direct us to the right tools. You would not think of trying to mend a car engine with a paint brush. But in the spiritual realm some Christians will try to paint a house with a wrench or mend a car engine with a paint brush. They seem to think that as long as they have a weapon, any weapon, they can use it for anything. The gifts of the Spirit are the equipment with which to get a job done. If we only knew that, and knew it in experience, how much more efficiently and accurately could jobs be done.

Be available to the Spirit

Often the Holy Spirit is unable to manifest himself in the way we need because we are simply not open or available to him for such a ministration. I am convinced that there are times when the Lord would very simply, in our times of prayer, be able to help us no end; but the problem is that no one is available. We think that because we are there for prayer, that is enough. We don't understand that there is equipment, there are tools for prayer; and if we are open and ready, then perhaps the Lord could use us.

In the same way, we need to widen the range of our availability to include any manifestation of the Spirit. Now you may be saying to yourself, 'Well, I don't know. I have not had any sensational and dramatic experience.' But don't let the enemy get hold of you. I have known many people who have come to me after a time of prayer and said things about a situation which have been a word of knowledge or a word of wisdom, but they never communicated it during the time of prayer. It was something which could have helped the whole time. If only we will make ourselves available to the Spirit, then such words could be communicated under the government of the Spirit.

Now I am not saying that we should just turn times of prayer into opportunities for the exercising of gifts. What I am saying is that if we will only be available, then there will be times when the Holy Spirit will be able to help us that little bit more and give us a greater clarity, uncover something for us, and enable us to go through. No gift can ever be exercised apart from the Holy Spirit. We need to know not only his indwelling and empowering; we need to be filled from day to day. That is another reason why we do not know any manifestation of the Spirit in our times of prayer. We are not being filled day by day. If we are, then he will stir up the gift that is within us.

Be willing to learn from mistakes

All gifts, every apparent manifestation of the Spirit, must be subject to the church. The rest of the members of the body must test and try everything of that order. What is of the Lord must be acted upon; what is not of the Lord must be rejected and left.

Now mistakes will be made; but if we all learn, there will be no harm, only progress. In every other sphere, we make mistakes, and who has not made a mistake in prayer? If you have opened your mouth in times of prayer, you must have made a mistake sometime. We all have. I have, you have; but it has not destroyed the whole work. We have learned from our mistakes and gone on. In the same way, who preaches and does not make a mistake? I do not know a single anointed preacher who has not made real mistakes in preaching. But we go on. Our whole ministry is not destroyed by mistakes that we make. We often learn a tremendous amount from them. Or what about the dreadful mistakes that have been made in witnessing? Just think of the terrible things we did when we were younger in the Lord. But the kingdom of heaven did not collapse. We came through; we are still here; and by the grace of God, we have learned.

In the same way we are bound to make mistakes in the exercise of gifts of the manifestation of the Spirit. But if we are prepared to learn and to go forward with the Lord,

then there will be minimal harm—the kind of harm that
the Holy Spirit can turn, in fact, into good.

However, when gifts are used to manipulate a group of
people or to impose someone's will or opinion, that is
falsehood and must be energetically rejected. If someone
continuously uses gifts in a wrong way, or in a soulish
manner, the responsible brethren should speak to that
person.

In a time of prayer, it is the purpose of that time which
governs the use of gifts. So if the purpose of this time of
corporate prayer is to get things done, then we are not all
going to speak in tongues at the top of our voices, as I
have heard in some places. They say, 'Well, of course, the
Lord understands it all.' But that is not corporate prayer.
Let us speak to the Lord in the language of devotion and
worship at home, and let the Lord use us in that way when
he wants to say something particular. But it is the purpose
and character of the time of prayer that must govern the
use of such gifts.

The basis is faith, not emotion

The manifestation of the Spirit is always through faith. We
need to be careful that we do not exercise a gift on the
basis of emotion or feeling. Some people seem to have the
idea that the only time you ever use a gift is when you are
engulfed with a wave of emotion and feeling, but the basis
for all the manifestation of the Spirit is faith, and faith
alone.

When you know God has given you a word, you may
have every doubt and fear in the world; then if you open
your mouth, it is faith. Do be careful of the idea that the
Holy Spirit manipulates you and you have to say certain
words. That is heathen. It has nothing to do with the Lord.
'The spirits of the prophets are subject to the prophets.'

Whenever the Holy Spirit really speaks through a person, even when that person cannot understand the full meaning of the words that he or she uses, they do hear and understand the words. Be clear on this because you will get people who tell you, 'I just had to do it; I was set on my feet and I had to do it.' That is not real inspiration at all. That is not faith. That is feeling, and therein lies great danger.

You may know you have got something from the Lord, you have some insight, then suddenly you are full of doubt and fear and you think to yourself, 'Don't be silly, you are going to make a fool of yourself. If you contribute that, they will all sit on you and that will be the end. And then you will go out and you will feel squashed.' But you can be sure by the very fact the enemy is trying to shut you up that there is some value in what God has given you. If you will only step forward in faith, then you will know a real manifestation of the Spirit. This is what happens with so many of us in prayer. Don't be afraid of that kind of emotion.

I remember the first time I prayed. I was very young. I was nearly paralysed. I felt something going up my neck, but it was not the Spirit of God, of course, it was just sheer fright. But in the end, I prayed, and I prayed in faith. And that is always how we have to.

Receive his speaking through Scripture

Many times, such manifestations of the Spirit come through some word of Scripture. Don't despise that, but honour it. Such contributions of Scripture, under the government of the Spirit, may be a word of knowledge or a word of wisdom or a word of prophecy and must be taken up and acted upon. We have certainly found again and again that the Lord has used this to show us the way ahead. Many things that I have been involved with have come about because the Lord spoke to us in times of prayer. Someone had a word on their heart and was able quietly to read it and did not try to follow it in prayer. It was just left to be judged by the rest. And so, when we knew it was the Lord, we were able to go forward. I just wish with all my heart that we could be more open in this matter and free from falsehood and counterfeit, and yet know in the most wonderful, spontaneous way this kind of manifestation of the Spirit in our times of prayer.

5

The Place of the Word of God in Prayer

And take the helmet of salvation, and the sword of the Spirit, which is the word of God: Praying always with all prayer and supplication in the Spirit, and watching thereunto with all perseverance and supplication for all saints (Ephesians 6:17–18).

For the word of God is quick, and powerful, and sharper than any twoedged sword, piercing even to the dividing asunder of soul and spirit, and of the joints and marrow, and is a discerner of the thoughts and intents of the heart (Hebrews 4:12).

And he had in his right hand seven stars: and out of his mouth went a sharp twoedged sword: and his countenance was as the sun shineth in his strength (Revelation 1:16).

For though we walk in the flesh, we do not war according to the flesh, for the weapons of our warfare are not of the flesh, but divinely powerful for the destruction of fortresses. We are destroying speculations and every lofty thing raised up against the knowledge of God, and we are taking every thought captive to the obedience of Christ (2 Corinthians 10:3–5, NASB).

For by Thee I can run upon a troop; and by my God I can leap over a wall. As for God, His way is blameless; the word of the Lord is tried; He is a shield to all who take refuge in

Him. For who is God, but the Lord? And who is a rock, except our God, the God who girds me with strength, and makes my way blameless? He makes my feet like hinds' feet, and sets me upon my high places. He trains my hands for battle, so that my arms can bend a bow of bronze. Thou hast also given me the shield of Thy salvation, and Thy right hand upholds me; and Thy gentleness makes me great. Thou dost enlarge my steps under me, and my feet have not slipped. I pursued my enemies and overtook them, and I did not turn back until they were consumed. I shattered them, so that they were not able to rise; they fell under my feet. For thou hast girded me with strength for battle; Thou hast subdued under me those who rose up against me (Psalm 18:29–39, NASB).

Blessed be the Lord my strength, which teacheth my hands to war, and my fingers to fight: My goodness, and my fortress; my high tower, and my deliverer; my shield, and he in whom I trust; who subdueth my people under me (Psalm 144:1–2).

This charge I commit unto thee, son Timothy, according to the prophecies which went before on thee, that thou by them mightest war a good warfare (1 Timothy 1:18).

We are in a warfare, and in this warfare, there are divinely provided weapons. True corporate prayer will always involve us in very real spiritual warfare and conflict. While there is an aspect of corporate prayer which is praise and thanksgiving, and there is an aspect which is inquiry of the Lord, there is also a major part which involves us in warfare and conflict.

We see that very clearly in the Scriptures. For example, we read in 2 Corinthians 10:3 that the weapons of our warfare are 'divinely powerful for the destruction of fortresses' (NASB).

The enemy has strong points. A fortress is not just a pretty little place; it is not a tourist spot. A fortress is a fortification. It is a strong place. And if that fortress falls, then a whole area is opened up to whoever takes the fortress. The word of God says that we are in a warfare and there are fortresses. It speaks about the demolition or destruction or, as the King James Version puts it, 'the pulling down of strongholds'. It also speaks of 'casting down imaginations'.

This word 'imaginations' is very interesting because it really means 'reasonings' or 'philosophical reasonings'. The New American Standard Bible has well translated it with the word 'speculations'. A tremendous amount of that which blinds people to the Lord Jesus Christ is speculation. Many things that people take absolutely for granted, as if they have been once and for all proved accurate, are in fact speculation. For example, the whole theory of evolution was based on speculation.

Whole sections of society are held in darkness and blindness by things which are, after all, speculative or philosophical reasonings, and the word of God says that these things are not just human; they are the result of spiritual powers that have injected ideas or imaginations into people; and those ideas are strong points in the enemy's fortification.

The so-called new morality is really one of these speculations, one of these philosophical reasonings. It seems to have so much to say for it, so much freedom to offer—a new way of life and all the rest of it—and it is beginning to hold more and more people in its grip. But it is a speculation. It is a stronghold of the enemy.

Verse 5 of 2 Corinthians 10 goes on to speak of 'every lofty thing raised up against the knowledge of God'. These are big things that contradict the word of God. They may appear to have so much in their support, so much evidence; but in fact they flatly contradict what God says. They are another strong point of Satan.

The New American Standard Version says that we are to take 'every thought captive to the obedience of Christ'.

Now isn't that a position of authority and power for the church of God, to be able to take every thought captive to obedience to Christ? Everything begins with a thought. Marxism began with a thought in a man called Karl Marx; Maoism began with the thoughts of Chairman Mao. We fail as the people of God if we accept all these thoughts as just physical and human reasonings and part of this fallen world and do not understand that there are things we can do about them. 'The weapons of our warfare are not of the flesh, but they are divinely powerful for the destruction of fortresses.' When we understand this we shall know what to do when we are up against these new movements, or policies that people have tried to push through Parliament and elsewhere.

The apostle Paul says in Ephesians 6, 'For our wrestling is not against flesh and blood, but against the principalities, against the powers, against the world-rulers of this darkness, against the spiritual hosts of wickedness in the heavenly places' (verse 12 RAV). Although we all accept that as Scripture, very few of us act as if we really believed it; for when it comes down to it, we believe that we are in fact up against flesh and blood. And if it is flesh and blood, then it has to be countered with the resources of flesh and blood. If it is an argument, counter it with argument. If it is a philosophy, counter it with philosophy. If it is art, counter it with art.

But the battle will never be won at any point by simply matching flesh and blood with flesh and blood. What lies behind the flesh and blood? That is exactly what the apostle is telling us: 'We wrestle not against flesh and blood'.

Just think of the hierarchy that is against us. We cannot simply discount our protagonists. We cannot just think of them as small minions in the satanic hierarchy. They are called principalities and rulers, powers and authorities.

They are world-rulers of this darkness. The darkness that blinds people to God and to Christ and to his salvation is something ruled by spiritual beings. It is not just coincidence; it is not something which finds its origin in flesh and blood. It is something which is ruled by spiritual beings behind the flesh and blood.

So there will be times when we take up a matter in prayer, for example as some of us did recently when we took up the whole educational scene in our country, and we will find that there are principalities and powers and a few world-rulers of this darkness sitting on top of our time of prayer. When we take up big matters, we get big spiritual beings interested. That is why Watchman Nee once said, 'Be very careful that you never over-reach yourself in the place of prayer.' It is possible to take up a matter that may be just too big. We must be together, we must be hidden, and we must know who our enemies are.

So for example if we decide to pray about the educational scene, there is a sense in which education will then be in the forefront of the warfare. Through it, the enemy is seeking to win the soul of a nation. He is seeking to capture a whole new generation for himself and to mould their thinking, their concepts, and their behaviour. If we take it up in prayer, therefore, we will be inviting the interests of higher-ups in the satanic hierarchy. But this is no reason to be afraid, for we have the armour of God.

I remember years ago, in a Sunday school time, a little boy read this out: 'That you may stand against the willies of the devil.' How wonderful when our praying can give the devil the willies! Then he will begin to fear and tremble because he knows that all we have to do is put on the Lord Jesus Christ in his entirety and stand. We do not have to go forward; we do not have to go backwards.

All we have to do is stand, withstand, and having done all, to stand; and the battle is ours. We will be so safe against principalities, powers, world-rulers of this darkness, hosts of wicked spirits. All we have to do is stand in Christ and the victory is ours.

The word 'wiles' means 'a scheme', 'a cunning device', 'craft', 'deceit'. Paul is saying that we will be able to stand against the deceits of the devil, the cunning devices of the devil, the schemes of the devil. Do we really think that the devil is someone with a tail and horns who runs around with a pronged fork? Do we think the devil is a dimwit, the biggest dimwit that was ever created, and that the simplest Christian can outwit him? My dear friends, the devil has supreme intelligence, next to God. Pride has made him blind, but he has a shrewdness and cunning and intelligence that is more than a match for all the believers put together—outside of Christ.

Do you think that we can just get together in prayer and utter a few petitions, and the whole front line of hell will collapse? The fact is that the devil gets wind of it before we have even started to pray and already has his plans. He may knock out some by bringing them home from work in such a state that they feel more crushed than alive. Someone else may get home to find that the tap is leaking, or the baby has been sick all day long, or there are five bills instead of the normal one. The result is that so many of us arrive at the time of prayer already knocked out, and with our heads full of other things. These are the cunning schemes of the enemy. 'Now,' he says to himself, 'I can sit on this whole time of prayer.'

Paul tells us that the armour is so that 'you may be able to withstand in the evil day' (verse 13). I am glad the Lord has put that in because not every day is an evil day, thank God. He keeps us out of the battle and protected for much of the time. But there are evil days, days of trouble, days when everything goes wrong. These are not necessarily periods of twenty-four hours, of course; just times when it seems as if all hell's pressure is suddenly exerted upon us.

In Ephesians 6:16 we see mention of the enemy's fiery darts. You know, some people sail through the big challenges, but the fiery dart gets them. They know that they are safe in Christ. They know what they are up against. But the devil just fires a fiery dart; it goes in between the armour, and they are finished, knocked out when they are most required in the battle. One of the weapons of Paul's day was the kind of dart that was covered with burning material; it was particularly injurious and destructive.

God provides weapons which spell victory

So we can see that in this matter of corporate prayer we are involved in warfare, in conflict. We are in very close proximity with the enemy. We must not be surprised if he gets hold of our corporate arm and twists it up our back, or if at times he sits upon us for a while so that we are pinned down and can hardly move. We are in a battle. But however fierce the warfare, God has provided us with the weapons which spell victory. So let us not just look at the warfare or the conflict. Let us remember that in the midst of this warfare, not discounting for one moment the power of our adversaries, God has given us weapons which spell victory.

What do these weapons of our warfare consist of? They consist in their entirety of truth. That is the only weapon God has given to the church: 'The sword of the Spirit which is the word of God.'

The only thing that can paralyse the enemy is truth. He is the father of lies. He was a liar from the beginning; and the one thing that shatters him is truth. He will laugh at anything else. But truth is the one thing that pierces right through and shatters him. It is the supreme weapon with which all the forces of evil can be destroyed.

How can we demolish the enemy's strong points? How can we destroy speculations and lofty things exalted against the knowledge of God and take every thought captive to the obedience of Christ? By truth; by the sword of the Spirit, which is the word of God. That is the only way that you and I can do it. The powers of darkness are never hurt by our words. We can talk for ever, and the devil will have a picnic while we go on. He has never been hurt by your words nor my words, even when they are biblical words. What we say does not do anything—not unless it is truth, the word of God.

The powers of darkness have never been hurt by our anger. I have heard people get so indignant and angry with the devil, but he is not hurt by that. I think he finds it rather funny when Christians get all angry and indignant. He is certainly not hurt by our much speaking or by our zeal. Some people get so zealous, so full of feeling about some matter, as if by their very emotion they are going to frighten the devil. But the enemy is never, at any single moment, hurt or even set back by our zeal or our feeling or our much speaking. In this warfare, the enemy is not even hurt by our biblical knowledge. You can know the Bible doctrinally from Genesis to Revelation but that will not give you an atom of authority when it comes to the enemy. There are many people I know who know their Bibles so well, but when it comes to really paralysing the powers of darkness, they are powerless.

Neither our correctness nor our sound doctrine (though that is necessary) nor our devotion has any power. The devil knows that he has only to get divine permission to take us into his care for a little while and our devotion would be undone within weeks. This is what he did with Job. All he has to do is to get divine protection removed from you and he could destroy you. He knows very well that your devotion will not help you, nor your biblical knowledge, nor your zeal.

The only thing which paralyses the forces of evil and destroys them is the truth—the word of God. Eternal reality shatters the powers of darkness and renders every satanic device inoperative. When truth is placed into our hands and we know how to use it in corporate prayer, then the enemy's devices will be useless. Do you believe that? There is not a device of Satan that cannot be rendered totally ineffective by truth.

Sometimes the youngest believer, providing he or she is covered, can use truth more effectively than an old saint who has lost his or her way. Why? Because they know very well that they have no great devotion, no biblical knowledge, and very little zeal with which to come against Satan, but they have got the truth. And when truth is used, every satanic device, whatever it is, is rendered ineffective and inoperative. Think of the power that God has given us as the body of Christ. What could we do if only we could see it and could allow the Spirit of God to teach us how to use it? It could transform our times of prayer.

Every strong point of Satan can be demolished by truth. Sometimes we think that if we get enough of us together and batter away at some strong point, then in the end, by sheer force of numbers, we will knock it down. But all we will do is wear ourselves out. The one thing that acts like a battering ram to demolish any stronghold or fortress of Satan is truth. And if you and I know how to use it and how to go on using it until the work is done, then strongholds will be demolished.

We have said that the weapons of our warfare are really the word of God—the truth. 'Thy word, O God, is truth,' said the Lord Jesus. So you can see how essential it is that we know the word of God in every way and have it dwelling in us. We need to get to know our Bibles, to memorise them, study them, and understand not just verses here and there but what is the underlying theme of what God has revealed in his word. But more importantly, we need the word of Christ to dwell in us so that it is not just biblical doctrine or themes, but the word of God which has come right into us and has become part of our flesh and blood. Even the youngest believer can start to know God's word and learn to use it in the battle.

Weapons are not produced, in the first place, for ornaments, but to be used. Nowadays we may hang on our wall swords or other weapons that are no longer in use, but we wouldn't hang up a Polaris missile, would we? Weapons are to be used for defence and offence; they are designed to protect, and to win battles. And God has provided the weapons of our warfare to protect us and to win battles.

We must all learn to use the sword of the Spirit. It is no good having a Bible if you do not know how to use it. How can you ever have a part in the administration of the kingdom of God in eternity if you have not first learned to use the word of God here?

Eternal facts to be used as weapons

The word of God is not philosophy; it is not speculation; it is not make-believe. The word of God is revealed truth. It is the revelation of eternal facts. Now here are some of the eternal facts which you and I ought to start using as the sword of the Spirit.

God is

God is. Not God was, nor God will be, but God *is*. That is the greatest weapon you can use in the battle against the enemy—God *is*. Do you understand what this means? God did not say, 'I have been that I have been,' or 'I shall be that I shall be,' or 'I was that I was.' He said, 'I am that I am.' God is 'I am'. And every single thing lives and moves and has its being in him, including the devil. What a weapon to use when suddenly you wake up to the fact that even the devil exists by the grace of God! God cannot be God unless everything exists in him. God *is*. God is love. God is life. God is light. Oh, what a weapon! When you look in the Bible—everywhere from Genesis to Revelation—you find this great eternal fact. It is a weapon with which you can paralyse Satan. When you say, 'God was,' Satan says, 'That's good; that is really good.' But when you start to recognise and proclaim, 'God *is*,' Satan is paralysed; because, though he is a liar, Satan always recognises truth.

The person of the Lord Jesus

'The Word became flesh and dwelt among us.' That is an eternal fact. We can speculate about the Lord Jesus and the person of the Lord Jesus; we can talk about him; but the fact of the matter is that God was manifest in the flesh. That is a fact; and that is why John the apostle said, 'Who is he that overcometh the world, but he that believeth that Jesus is the Son of God?' (1 John 5:5). I used to read that verse and think: What does that have to do with over-coming the world? I could not see the connection. Now I see that it is foundational to overcoming the world. It is an eternal fact.

The finished work of Christ

Here is an eternal fact. It is not make-believe; it is not a possibility; it is not some vague hope we have, that by his death we might be saved. Here is something which is eternal fact. Through his redemption, he saves every man or woman who will humble himself or herself and come to God through him. And through that finished work, Jesus has beaten the powers of darkness. The Lord Jesus said, 'Now is the prince of this world cast out'; and he said it just before going to the cross. How Satan hates it when we use the finished work of Jesus Christ as our weapon! 'The Son of God was manifested that he might destroy the works of the devil' (see 1 John 3:8b). When you take the finished work of Jesus Christ, instantly Satan is paralysed; and he knows it. It is an eternal fact. He has stripped principalities and powers naked, triumphing openly over them through his cross (see Colossians 2:15).

The present position of Christ

Here is another eternal fact: at this moment Jesus is King of kings and Lord of lords and Head over all things to the church. He is ruler of the kings of the earth. All the rulers, all the presidents, all the kings reign by the grace of God and the permission of our Lord Jesus. That is the fact. The present position of our Lord Jesus is a tremendous weapon. The Most High rules in the affairs of men.

The immutability of his counsel

We must learn to use the word of God not only as the revelation of eternal facts, but we must use it because it is and it contains the immutability of his counsel. It is the revelation of the counsel of God, which is immutable. Now this word 'immutable' means 'unchangeable, no possibility of deviation'. 'Wherein God, willing more abundantly to shew unto the heirs of promise the immutability of his counsel . . .' (Hebrews 6:17). 'Being born again, not of corruptible seed, but of incorruptible, by the word of God, which liveth and abideth for ever. For all flesh is as grass, and all the glory of man as the flower of grass. The grass withereth, and the flower thereof falleth

away: But the word of the Lord endureth for ever' (1 Peter
1:23–25). 'Every good gift and every perfect gift is from
above, and cometh down from the Father of lights, with
whom is no variableness, neither shadow of turning'
(James 1:17). The immutability of his counsel: that
means that what is in this book is unchangeable. God
has given us his counsel and he is not going to deviate
from it. He has given his word and he is going to keep to
it. Up to this moment, God has fulfilled every single thing
that he has ever said would happen in world history.
Therefore, we know that he who promised is faithful.

What has God said about world history? He has said
that it is heading for judgement. What has God said about
world history? He has said that Jesus will come. What has
God said about Israel? He has said that not only will Israel
come together again, as she has, but that she will survive
and finally turn to God. This is the counsel of the Lord. It
never changes. Now that is a weapon, and Satan knows it;
and when you begin to use a weapon like that, he is
paralysed.

The promises of God

We must learn to use the promises made over to us. 'For
as many as may be the promises of God, in Him they are
yes; wherefore also by Him is our Amen to the glory of
God through us' (2 Corinthians 1:20, NASB). In Hebrews
10:23, there is a lovely little phrase: '. . . for he is faithful
that promised.' What a beautiful little word! Or again, we
find this one in 2 Peter 1:4: 'Whereby are given unto us
exceeding great and precious promises: that by these ye
might be partakers of the divine nature.' That means every
time you take a promise and stand upon it and see it
fulfilled, there is something more of the Lord in you.

You often see the promises of God stuck up all over

people's walls, especially in the bathroom. But when it comes down to it, none of us really expects them to work. We think we need to use common sense. I once learned otherwise.

Aunt Ella used to give my sister singing lessons. Now most people thought Aunt Ella was a bit crazy. She talked so fast that I remember the pastor once saying, 'I do thank God that he can unravel her prayers.' She spoke beautiful English, but she talked so fast that no one could understand her. I would go up and walk home with my sister when she had finished her singing lesson. I was just thirteen at the time, having only been saved a year. On this day, my sister had already left when I arrived, and Auntie Ella and I got to talking. She was sewing something and we were talking about the Lord, when something went wrong with the sewing machine. She tried various things, and then she asked me if I knew anything about sewing machines. I didn't, but I had a go at it and it seemed to me to be absolutely jammed.

Then she said something I have never forgotten: 'Now we must ask our heavenly Father.' She knelt down and she made me kneel down with the sewing machine before us. I will never forget her prayer. Her hand went out and she said: 'Heavenly Father, Lance and I have been having such a lovely time of fellowship about your beloved Son. As you know, I am not a very practical lady.' (She had been an opera singer and had had everything done for her for most of her life.) 'Something has gone wrong with this sewing machine. I tried to put it right, but I am an old lady and I do not understand anything about sewing machines. And Lance, dear boy, has tried to put it right, but he has not been able to do anything. Heavenly Father, you say in your word, in 2 Corinthians 1:20, "For as many as may be the promises of God, in him they are yes; wherefore also by him is our Amen to the glory of God through us." I want to bring to you a promise from Hebrews 1:14, that the angels are sent forth to minister to those who are the heirs of salvation. Heavenly Father, will you please send an angel to put this sewing machine right.'

With that, she bowed her head. I had my eyes wide open, and I touched her on the arm and said, 'Auntie, try the machine again.'

'Shhh. Give the angel time.' She knelt there with her head bowed for a minute or two and then she got up, drew her chair under the sewing machine and went straight on with her sewing, saying, 'Oh, heavenly Father, you never fail; thank you so much.'

Now, of course, I was only thirteen, but I had heard all sorts of people, well-known people, in the pulpit. They never really meant too much to me other than that they gave marvellous messages. I never expected much of what they said to work, and I don't think anyone else did either.

I always told Auntie Ella that she taught me one simple thing—that you can take a promise of God's word on the basis of what he himself has said and put it to the test. From then on, every time we sang the old hymn 'Standing on the promises of Christ my King' I knew what it meant.

The Spirit's direction

How do we use the weapons of our warfare in corporate prayer? It is not enough to *know* the word of God. It is not even enough to have *memorised* the word of God. It is through the Spirit alone that we can *use* the word of God effectively in prayer. It is 'the sword of the Spirit'. That doesn't just mean that he is the author of the word of God. It does mean that, of course—he is the inspirer of every single part of it. But it also means that only the Spirit can direct us as to how to use the word of God. We cannot just suddenly take some scripture that we have memorised and

say, 'Now I am going to use it.' Something has to be
kindled in our heart, and at that instant, the sword of the
Spirit is in our hand.

We read in Psalm 18 where David talked about his
hands being trained to war and he said, 'I pursued them
and I did not turn back until I shattered them.' Many times
in prayer, people turn back before they have shattered the
enemy. Then the enemy recovers to deal them a terrible
blow. We have to learn that once we have taken up a
matter, we are to carry it through. That does not mean
in one evening necessarily. There are times when the Holy
Spirit seems to say, 'Drop the matter and leave it till
next week.' But we must not take up a matter and then
leave it half done. We need the Holy Spirit to lead us to
the exact weapon in God's word, the truth which we
have to use and with which this particular battle can
be won. Therefore, we need to be open to the Spirit's
ministry in this way.

The Lord has to train us. David said: 'He has trained me
for war and taught my fingers how to fight.' We have to
learn these things. 'He trains my hands for battle so that
my arms can bend a bow of bronze' (see Psalm 18:34).
That sort of strength does not come overnight. People
have to train to bend a bow of bronze.

'Thou hast girded me with strength unto the battle'
(verse 39). 'It is God that girdeth me with strength, and
maketh my way perfect' (see verse 32). The Lord does all
this. The Lord is the one who trains and teaches and
instructs and enables us. He girds us with strength for
the battle.

And then in verse 29, it says, 'For by thee I have run
through a troop.' How wonderful when we can surprise a
whole troop of the enemy.

The will of God

There are times when we can use the will of God in this warfare like Daniel (see Daniel 9). By the Spirit of the Lord, Daniel discovered when the seventy years of captivity began. And in that sense, he was far more with it than many theologians since, because there has always been controversy about the seventy years' captivity. In actual fact, the people of God were only in Babylon for fifty years. But the Spirit of God showed Daniel when the seventy years began.

Now, because the Spirit of God showed him that through the prophecy of Jeremiah, the prophet, Daniel had a sword in his hand. He had the sword of the Spirit in his hand, and he went to prayer; and he refused to stop until the thing came to pass. When we know the whole way that the book of Daniel is built—the first six chapters and the last six chapters—we discover to our amazement that Daniel's going into the lions' den coincided with the setting of his face towards Jerusalem three times a day in prayer. In other words, many people thought that Daniel was crazy, but not the devil. The one being in the universe who knew that Daniel's prayer meant a tremendous amount was the enemy. And he put it into the heads of those evil dignitaries and government officers to go to the emperor and get a law passed that no one should pray to anyone but the emperor for a month. And when the enemy had done that, he thought he had won the day. But Daniel went on praying. The enemy then thought he would defeat Daniel by getting him put into the lions' den. Now it was the turn of heaven to be perturbed and disturbed. I can imagine the question in heaven: 'Should we bring Daniel home via the lions or do we shut the lions' mouths?'

And it was as if God said, 'It is more important to us here that Daniel stays. You can bring all the rest of the people of God home by the lions, but not Daniel. Daniel has seen something and he is praying something into being. You give him faith so that he is able to go into that lions' den and find that the mouths of the lions are shut up.' And of course, that is exactly what happened. Daniel came out of the lions' den; and all the people who had been against him were themselves fed to the lions. Daniel went on with his prayer ministry until he saw the people of God go back. He overlived the return to Jerusalem and to Israel by three years.

Daniel knew the will of God. In our day, we rarely hear people using the will of God in this general way. But there are things that God has revealed that are going to come to pass; and those are the things we can stand upon and use as weapons.

It says in the word of God: 'If any man see his brother sin a sin which is not unto death, he shall ask, and he shall give him life for them that sin not unto death.' But it says expressly: 'There is a sin unto death: I do not say that he shall pray for it' (1 John 5:16). We can know the will of God specifically about a matter.

For example, here is a promise of the Lord in Proverbs: 'Trust in the Lord with all thine heart; and lean not unto thine own understanding. In all thy ways acknowledge him, and he shall direct thy paths' (Proverbs 3:5–6). If we fulfil the conditions, God will fulfil the promise. That is a promise. 'My God shall supply all your need according to his riches in glory by Christ Jesus' (Philippians 4:19). There are so many promises, and only the Holy Spirit can lead us to them.

Sometimes, the word of God interprets the situation. I remember years ago being struck by a story about that great Danish servant of the Lord, Pastor Fjord Christensen. A group of people were called out into the country to pray for a woman who had not been able to walk for a number of years because she was crippled with arthritis. But she was a believer and so was her husband. As they prayed and prayed, a younger man prayed with much zeal and much devotion, but he did not get far. The older man, Fjord Christensen, just said 'Amen' at different points and kept very quiet. He was looking in his Bible. Suddenly, he stopped the prayer and said to the lady, 'Could you tell me, are you short-tempered?'

She was startled and said, 'Oh, no!'

So they continued to pray. Then a little later, he stopped again and said, 'Excuse me asking, but are you quite sure that you are not irritable?'

'Oh no, never,' she said. 'I never get irritated.'

So they went on praying. Suddenly, he said, 'Are you absolutely certain that you are not short-tempered?'

And when she was about to say 'no', her husband burst in with tears in his eyes and said, 'Oh, but you are! You are! It is the worst thing about you.'

'Ah,' said Fjord Christensen, 'I thought so.'

The woman burst into tears and she confessed to the Lord how short-tempered she was with her husband and everything else. When it was all out of her and she had really repented, Fjord Christensen said, 'Now we can ask the Lord to heal you.' And he read her Proverbs 14:30 which in Danish is translated 'A sound heart is the life of the flesh: but short-temperedness is the rottenness of the bones.'

While they had been praying, this verse had come to Fjord Christensen, and that is why he persisted in his questions until the truth was revealed. When they laid hands on that woman, she stood up and was able to see the men out. She lived a normal life until her death, and never had arthritis again.

Now that is what I mean by 'the sword of the Spirit, which is the word of God'. They could have gone round and round that situation, praying for healing and never touching the root of it, because the root of it was that short-temperedness was causing the arthritis. When that was understood, instantly God touched it. (Please note that I am not saying that every single case of arthritis is caused by irritability; so don't come under condemnation.) The word of the Lord came into that situation through a faithful servant of God and Satan did not have a chance of keeping that woman bound, not for another day, once she saw it and repented of it.

When the Spirit of God has brought some Scripture into the prayer time, we need to take it up and use it as the Lord directs us. Battles are won or lost in the measure by which we respond to leadership and are related to one another. So often, when someone is given a scripture which is the sword of the Spirit in that situation, the rest of us fail to respond.

Practical points

I am always amazed when people come to a time of prayer without a Bible. Always bring your Bible to a time of prayer; never be without it.

Second, use the word of God as led and directed by the Spirit in the prayer time. We can only learn how by experience.

Third, be alive and sensitive to the Spirit; watch and pray. Follow the whole time. Don't just doze or be lost in your own thoughts. Sometimes, you see a person looking completely lost in their own thoughts. The next moment, they are praying. Is it any wonder that their prayers are not related to anything that has gone before or after? We need to keep alert.

Avoid sermonettes, Bible precis, Bible outlines, or preaching at God. That is not using the sword of the

Spirit. People have got the idea that, because they feel they must use the word of God, they can give a Bible outline and Satan will be frightened. He is not frightened at all. But he is frightened when the Holy Spirit helps you to take the word of God and use it directly, not as a little sermon.

When the Lord gives you a verse or a passage from his word during the prayer time, read it distinctly when you contribute it. Do not feel that you must follow such a contribution immediately with prayer. It is often good to let others weigh the passage first.

Only read the relevant verse or verses, not the whole chapter. Time is too precious for that.

Then once we have discovered the weapon, we need to use it. Sometimes, it does not take so long; other times, it will be a long battle. The government of the Spirit will decide how long we have to use that weapon.

Lastly, a truth or a promise needs to be stood upon, not only by the person who contributed it by the Spirit, but by everyone present. Sometimes, when a word comes and someone really claims something, we all think, 'Oh, that's wonderful.' And that's that. A time of prayer is an expression of the body of Christ. No one is giving anything that is personal. The whole time is the expression of our mutuality, and if God gives someone a promise, it is for us all. If God gives direction, it is for us all. If a manifestation of the Spirit comes, it is for us all, and we need to learn how to take it up and really use it together.

6

Executing the Will of God in Prayer

Praise ye the Lord. Sing unto the Lord a new song, and his praise in the congregation of saints. Let Israel rejoice in him that made him: let the children of Zion be joyful in their King. Let them praise his name in the dance: let them sing praises unto him with the timbrel and harp. For the Lord taketh pleasure in his people: he will beautify the meek with salvation. Let the saints be joyful in glory: let them sing aloud upon their beds. Let the high praises of God be in their mouth, and a twoedged sword in their hand; To execute vengeance upon the heathen, and punishments upon the people; To bind their kings with chains, and their nobles with fetters of iron; To execute upon them the judgment written: this honour have all his saints. Praise ye the Lord (Psalm 149:1–9).

O clap your hands, all peoples; shout to God with the voice of joy. For the Lord Most High is to be feared, A great King over all the earth. He subdues peoples under us, And nations under our feet. He chooses our inheritance for us, the glory of Jacob whom he loves. God has ascended with a shout, The Lord, with the sound of a trumpet. Sing praises to God, sing praises; sing praises to our King, sing praises. For God is the King of all the earth; sing praises with a skilful psalm. The princes of the people have assembled themselves as the people of the God of Abraham; For the shields of the earth belong to God; He is highly exalted (Psalm 47:1–9, NASB).

103

Just notice the tense through the Psalm: 'He subdues peoples under us. He is a great King over all the earth. He subdues peoples under us, nations under our feet. God reigneth over the nations. God sitteth upon His holy throne.'

'The shields of the earth'—that means all the victories, because they brought the shields back to hang in the house of the Lord. That means all the victories belong to the Lord.

> It is better to trust in the Lord than to put confidence in man. It is better to trust in the Lord than to put confidence in princes [that is the most educated of men]. All nations compassed me about: but in the name of the Lord will destroy them. They compassed me about; yea, they compassed me about: but in the name of the Lord will I destroy them. They compassed me about like bees; they are quenched as the fire of thorns: for in the name of the Lord I will destroy them. Thou hast thrust sore at me that I might fall: but the Lord helped me. The Lord is my strength and song, and is become my salvation. The voice of rejoicing and salvation is in the tabernacles of the righteous: the right hand of the Lord doeth valiantly. The right hand of the Lord is exalted: the right hand of the Lord doeth valiantly. I shall not die, but live, and declare the works of the Lord (Psalm 118:8–17).

Now will you notice that all these nations that surround the psalmist, he cuts off in the name of the Lord. And then we have this extraordinary statement: 'The right hand of the Lord doeth valiantly.' So when he cuts them off with his right hand, the right hand of the Lord doeth valiantly. In other words, the right hand of the Lord will not come in until he uses his right hand in faith. Now when you are surrounded by all the nations, you may feel you are a minority. And therefore, you might as well give up and let the Lord come in sovereignly and do something instead of you. But the Lord will not do it. Until you cut them off in the name of the Lord, the right hand of the Lord does not do valiantly. But the moment you act in faith, then according to the will of God, the right hand of the Lord doeth valiantly.

> The Lord said unto my Lord, Sit thou at my right hand, until I make thine enemies thy footstool. The Lord shall send the rod of thy strength out of Zion: rule thou in the midst of thine enemies. Thy people shall be willing in the day of thy power in the beauties of holiness.

Now notice that he says to the Messiah, 'Sit thou at my right hand, until I make thine enemies thy footstool.' Now who under God and through the sovereign power and direction of the Spirit of God makes those enemies the footstool of the Lord Jesus? They do not just become the footstool of the Lord Jesus willy-nilly. It is through the church that one after another of these principalities and powers are vanquished and put where they belong—under the feet of the Lord Jesus Christ. And we have to do it. It is as simple as that. 'Rule thou in the midst of thine enemies' (Psalm 110:1–3a).

> Verily I say unto you [plural], Whatsoever ye shall bind on earth shall be bound in heaven: and whatsoever ye shall loose on earth shall be loosed in heaven. Again I say unto you, That if two of you shall agree on earth as touching any thing that they shall ask, it shall be done for them of my Father which is in heaven. For where two or three are gathered together in my name, there am I in the midst of them (Matthew 18:18–20).

> No man can enter into a strong man's house, and spoil his goods, except he will first bind the strong man; and then he will spoil his house (Mark 3:27).

In this chapter I want to consider the matter of executive prayer. What do I mean by 'executive prayer'? I mean the kind of corporate prayer by which the purpose of God is carried out or executed in the secret place before it is publicly manifested.

The word 'executive' means 'a person or body with the power to execute specific policies'. We speak sometimes of the government executive, which is a body that has the right to carry out the policies of the government. It comes from the word 'execute' which means 'to follow through, or to carry into effect'.

When we speak of a business executive we mean that he is not a clerk or even a manager; he is more than that. He is someone who has authority to sign on behalf of the administration or the company. If you need something, he is someone who can get things done. Another way of looking at it is that an executive is someone who 'executes' the policy of the board of directors. An executive is someone with authority.

Now we are all executives of the kingdom of God. This is the wonderful thing about being a child of God. That may seem very odd to you, and it is certainly a bit abnormal to find that every single person in the company of the kingdom of God is an executive. But that is exactly what our Lord means when he speaks of us as kings. We have been authorised in the name of Christ, who is the Head of the church, to carry out the policy of his kingdom, to put into effect the decrees of the throne of God. Whatever God has decreed, you and I have been authorised to carry into effect. We have been made executives in the sense that we are to see that the policy of the kingdom of God is put into effect here on earth as it is in heaven.

'And hath made us kings and priests unto God and his Father; to him be glory and dominion for ever and ever' (Revelation 1:6). He made us to be kings and priests. Some versions render this 'He has made us a kingdom,' and the thought there is that we are not just a territory ruled over, but a kingship, an executive body with the right to carry out the policies of heaven.

'And hast made [us] unto our God kings and priests: and we shall reign on the earth' (Revelation 5:10). The verse does not say, 'They shall reign upon the earth.' It is in the present tense: 'They reign upon the earth.' These people have been bought out of every kindred and tribe and tongue and nation and have been made a people unto God—priests and kings unto God. They are to reign upon this earth.

'And hath raised us up [together], and made us sit together in heavenly places in Christ Jesus' (Ephesians 2:6). What does that mean, unless it means that we are to reign with him now? We are enthroned with him. We have come to a place of ascendancy. It is not only that we have been made alive together with Christ, we have not only been raised from the dead (which means we have ascended) but we are 'made us sit together in heavenly places'.

'Which he wrought in Christ, when he raised him from the dead, and set him at his own right hand in the heavenly places, Far above all principality, and power, and might, and dominion, and every name that is named, not only in this world, but also in that which is to come' (Ephesians 1:20–21). That is a pretty exhaustive list. All rule. That includes everything.

'And he hath put all things under his feet, and gave him to be the head over all things to the church, Which is his body' (verse. 22).

Where are you in all this? You are in him. You are between the Head and the feet. We have been made kings and priests unto God. Kings are executives carrying out the laws and decrees of the kingdom. They see that the laws and decrees of their kingdom are carried out to the full; they are executives.

Authority

Now for us this executive authority is contained in the phrase 'in the name of Jesus'. 'Again I say unto you, That if two of you shall agree on earth as touching any thing that they shall ask, it shall be done for them of my Father which is in heaven. For where two or three are gathered together in my name, there am I in the midst of them' (Matthew 18:19–20).

'Wherefore God also hath highly exalted him, and given him a name which is above every name: That at the name of Jesus every knee should bow, of things in heaven, and things in earth, and things under the earth' (Philippians 2:9–10).

This does not just mean that one day all this is going to happen. It means that even now all principalities and powers and demons are subject to the Lord Jesus Christ.

The name of the Lord speaks of authority. When a woman marries a man, she takes his name, and that name is her authority. She can go to the bank and say, 'I am Mrs So and So,' and that is her authority to draw out the money. Whenever we meet together, or pray together, or act together, we are to do it all in the name of the Lord Jesus. The Scriptures tell us that if we ask the Father in his name, he will give it to us. There is our authority.

'Fear not; I am the first and the last: I am he that liveth, and was dead, and behold, I am alive for evermore . . . and have the keys of hell and death' (Revelation 1:17b–18). Before John was to see those terrible visions, those revelations of the power and might of Satan and of the beast and of the false prophet and all those other things, he was first to see that the Lord Jesus has not only the keys of heaven but the keys of death and hell. They are all in the hands of the risen Christ.

Keys symbolise authority

You give keys to people you can trust. You invest them with authority because, by giving them keys, they can get into things and they can get out of things. They can lock things up and they can unlock things. That is authority. Someone who can lock or unlock a door has authority. Not everyone can do it. Only the person who has got the key can unlock the door and lock it again. So keys symbolise authority.

Keys are such simple things; most people have some of them. They are just little pieces of metal cut in certain ways, some of them so small they are hardly worth thinking about. We use them unthinkingly, automatically. You never think about them until you lose them—and then your troubles begin. What was so simple and so quick becomes complex, awkward, and difficult. You go rushing around. Can you find a phone? Have you got change for the phone? Is the person in that you are going to phone? 'Can you help me? I have lost my keys.'

I believe the church has mislaid the keys of the kingdom. Things that were once so simple are now complex, involved, and difficult. There was a time when the church got down to prayer and things happened—not always immediately; but things happened—because they had the keys of the kingdom. Now everything seems so difficult and complicated. We have lost our keys, and somehow or other, we need to deal with this. Oh, what a need there is for executive prayer in our day and generation!

We all believe, if it is only in the head, that we are surrounded by spiritual powers and the fact is that we need to rediscover the keys of the kingdom. We need to lock up the powers of darkness and unlock the captives who are in their grip.

We are meant not only to inquire of the Lord and

earnestly seek him—we are not only to pour out our hearts
before him—but we are meant in the name of Christ to
take action in the secret place of prayer; to use the keys of
the kingdom. Our Lord taught us in the pattern prayer to
pray: 'Thy kingdom come. Thy will be done in earth, as it
is in heaven' (Matthew 6:10). This is a declaration, not a
plea. It is not 'Please let thy kingdom come; please let thy
will be done on earth as it is in heaven.' There is no 'let'.
'Thy kingdom come!' is a declaration. The Lord Jesus said
to his disciples, 'Go out two by two in my name and say to
them the kingdom of God has come to you.' It is what he
has told us to declare to the world: 'The kingdom of God
is come.'

> And Simon Peter answered and said, Thou art the Christ, the
> Son of the living God. And Jesus answered and said unto
> him, Blessed art thou, Simon Bar-jona: for flesh and blood
> hath not revealed it unto thee, but my Father which is in
> heaven. And I say also unto thee, That thou art Peter [that is,
> a little splinter of rock], and upon this rock [that is, the
> bedrock] I will build my church; and the gates of hell shall
> not prevail against it. And I will give unto thee the keys of
> the kingdom of heaven: and whatsoever thou shalt bind on
> earth shall be bound in heaven: and whatsoever thou shalt
> loose on earth shall be loosed in heaven (Matthew 16:16–19).

It appears that the building work of Christ and his clear
statement about the forces of evil not prevailing against
his church are related to our use of the keys of the kingdom.
In other words, it is as if the Lord is saying to us that if we
use the keys of the kingdom of heaven, the building work
will go on and nothing that hell can do will prevail. But if
we do not use the keys of the kingdom of heaven, the
whole building operation will be paralysed.

If we look at church history, we discover evidence of
this. Every time there was a surge of activity in the building

of the house of God, we discover that there were men and women who were able to use the keys of the kingdom of heaven. Every God-sent, Holy Spirit revival has been accompanied by executive action on the part of the members of the body of Christ.

Opening the gates

'Thou art Peter, and upon this rock I will build my church; and the gates of hell shall not prevail against it. I will give unto thee the keys of the kingdom of heaven.'

Here we come to another wonderful thing; and this is why I am such a firm believer in the authority and the inspiration of the word of God, no matter what kind of problem people have with the word of God. It is amazing to me that when you get ambiguity, it is nearly always because the Lord, in his great wisdom, wants to include two thoughts in one verse. And this is what you have here in this word 'shall not prevail against it'. The word is 'shall not be strong or powerful against it'. This means that the powers of darkness will not destroy the building work of Christ by overwhelming it; they will not prevail against it; they will not overcome it. And the other thought is that they will not be able to hold out against the church's offensive. 'Upon this rock I will build my church, and the gates of hell shall not hold out against it.' That is the other interpretation; but I think both are right. First of all, if we use the keys, we can lock up the gates of hell so that they cannot come out in that way to overwhelm the building work of the Lord Jesus Christ. But within those gates, there are multitudes of captives whom the Lord Jesus would bring out and make part of his building work; but until you and I have unlocked the gates of hell, they cannot come out.

In other words, we can evangelise and evangelise, but

until we learn how to use the keys, Satan will make sure those gates are kept shut to keep in the people who should be coming out. Again and again, we have run into blockades. What are they? It is as if Satan has said: 'Shut the gates! Shut the gates! Too many are getting out.' We do not know what has happened. All we know is that, suddenly, people do not get saved. There are no people coming out. And if we are not careful, we turn in on one another. We will say: 'So and so was wrong. It was this; it was the preaching; we should have done this, or we should do that.' The actual fact is all we have to do is get behind the scenes and use the keys. We have authority. There is not a person whom the Lord cannot bring out once we use the authority that is given to us.

What is the supreme weapon of Satan? It is death. He keeps men and women in bondage all of their lifetime through fear of death. His great weapon is spiritual death. He tries to destroy every single work of God by imposing death on it. His supreme weapon is death. 'Upon this rock, I will build my church; and the gates of hell [the powers of death] shall not prevail against it.' He will neither be able to keep captives in bondage through fear of death, nor will he be able to impose death upon the building work of the Lord Jesus Christ.

This is ground for the prayer warriors to take up things. Every time we find death is coming in, it is something to be thankful for. The enemy is up in arms, seeking to impose something upon us, seeking to destroy something that is of God with death. We have keys in this matter. We can unlock these gates of death and let out people who are trapped in it. We can lock up these gates when it is an imposition upon the building work of our Lord Jesus Christ.

We know very well that when people have been saved, that is only the beginning of the battle. The battle is to get people built up into the house of God. All kinds of issues come up and many of us get so worn out trying to face those issues; and so we will be worn out until we learn to use the keys. If we would learn to use the keys behind the scenes, we would see a good deal more building up. We would not put up with this work of the enemy bringing fragmentation and disintegration and deterioration and death. If we had just a little bit of spiritual guts about us, we would start to stand up in the name of the Lord and use the keys that have been given to us in this matter.

Gates symbolise power

In Scripture, because of their importance and their protective strength, gates symbolise power. In the good old days there was not a city that did not have huge walls and gates, and when those gates were closed, no one could get in. I remember my great uncle, who lived all his life in that amazing city, Peking, telling me about going out to play golf in a club outside the city. While he was gone, an old warlord came up against the warlord who was in charge of Peking, and they had a fight. So the warlord in charge of Peking closed the gates, and for three months, no one got in. My uncle lived inside the golf club for three months; but it was a very sophisticated golf club, so he liked it. But can you imagine such a thing—some old warlord saying, 'Shut the gates!' and the gates were shut? Peking has three great solid walls, one right after another, and when the gates were shut, that was the end of the matter.

Until a century or two ago, all the cities of Europe had walls and gates. Those gates were strategically important because that was the way in and out. They were the protective strength. It was no good having a great wall if the gates could be battered in. The whole point of the gates was that they were not only the way in and the way out, but they could be closed and kept closed. Otherwise there was no point in the fortification.

Gates symbolise counsel

Therefore, in the Scripture, gates symbolise power. But they symbolise more than power. Do you remember how in the Old Testament it often speaks about the elders sitting in the gates? Why? In the old days, these gates were very big and cavernous, and they provided shade and cool. They were, of course, a great community centre point for the whole city. It was there that the elders held court and administered law. It was there that the decisions were made. It was there that anyone could come with a complaint and receive some kind of adjudication or arbitration. Gates thus came to symbolise counsel, judgement and policy. And now we have something tremendous. 'Upon this rock I will build my church, and the counsel of hell shall not prevail against it.' Let me put it another way: the policy of the powers of darkness will not be achieved or carried into effect against the building work of the Lord Jesus Christ. Put it another way: the judgement, the plan, the purpose of Satan will not prevail against the building work of the Lord Jesus.

The whole danger in saying this is that you think that is enough: 'Thank God that Jesus said, "Upon this rock I will build my church, and the gates of hell shall not prevail against it."' But the Lord said to Peter: 'I have given thee the keys of the kingdom of heaven: and whatsoever thou shalt loose on earth shall be loosed in heaven; and whatsoever thou shalt bind on earth shall be bound in heaven.' In other words, the counsel of hell *will* prevail unless you use the keys. The judgement of Satan will prevail. He will bring about disintegration. He will come in like a flood and overwhelm everything. He will destroy every bit of building work unless you and I as the people of God rise up and use the keys.

It is no good saying that every single matter of prayer has got to have executive action; the Holy Spirit has to direct us. But sometimes, you feel sick when you hear someone ask the Lord to do something but their prayer is never carried into action. There is no using of the keys. And Satan laughs: 'Look at those silly people, spending all that time on their knees. Don't they understand that until they take action, nothing can be done?'

Thus we have the kingdom of heaven, the gates of hell, and the building work of Christ. The gates of hell will prevail unless we learn to use the keys.

> I will give unto thee the keys of the kingdom of heaven: and whatsoever thou shalt bind on earth shall be bound in heaven: and whatsoever thou shalt loose on earth shall be loosed in heaven (Matthew 18:19).

The New American Standard Bible is the only version that has attempted accurately to convey the meaning of that verse. It is not that you and I say we are going to bind this and heaven agrees to ratify it; or we are going to loose something and heaven agrees to do it. Rather, it is because our risen Lord is in the midst by the Holy Spirit, and we are gathered in his name, that agreement comes into us. There is a witness of the Spirit in this matter that such and such has got to be done about it. That takes us back to Matthew 18:19–20: 'Again I say unto you, That if two of you shall agree on earth as touching any thing that they shall ask, it shall be done for them of my Father which is in heaven. For where two or three are gathered together in my name, there am I in the midst of them.' In other words, you cannot bind anything that heaven does not will to be bound; you cannot loose anything that heaven does not will to be loosed. But once we know the mind of our risen Lord, of our risen Head, by the Spirit of God, then we only have to utter the words and it is done.

We are carrying out the decrees of heaven. Everywhere in the Bible we see this illustrated. For example, take Moses. Do you think that Moses just suddenly said, 'Oh dear, all of us have got to get across the Red Sea, but the only way to do it is to split it open. So if I lift up the rod and say an authoritative word, heaven will fall in with me'? Not so! The Lord said to Moses, 'Do this thing.' 'Lift thou up thy rod, and stretch out thy hand over the sea, and divide it' (Ex 14:16). Fancy the Lord saying to Moses, 'You divide the Red Sea.' It really is laughable, isn't it? Moses knew very well that he was not dividing the Red Sea.

But the point is that if Moses had refused to lift up the rod and stretch out his hand and say the authoritative word over the Red Sea, it would have remained as impassable a sea as it ever had been. The people never would have gone across. The sovereignty of God was not going to work until Moses himself uttered the decree of heaven over that sea. Until God can get hold of us as the members of Christ's body and of our human lips to utter on earth the decree that has already been passed in heaven, God will not do it.

When the priests carried the ark into the river Jordan, it was not that they said, 'We are going in here and we expect you, Lord, to follow us and do something on our behalf.' No! The Lord had told them that wherever they put the soles of their feet, it would be theirs. They were told to go into the river Jordan and stand there; and that is exactly what they did. When they got their feet wet, the river stood up in a heap quite a few miles upstream. But it was the decree of heaven that those people should get across into the land; therefore, whatsoever they bound on earth had already been bound in heaven. It was as if heaven said, 'This Jordan is bound.' But it was not bound; not until the children of God on earth with their feet on the actual soil said, 'It is bound! In the name of our God, it is bound.' Then heaven said, 'Right; it is done!' And it was done.

Our Lord put it in very simple words when he said that if we are to enter the strong man's house and spoil his goods, we must first bind him (see Mark 3:27). It is the missing link in evangelism. I have never failed to be amazed at so many evangelistic efforts which fail to understand that unless we get behind the scenes first and bind the strong man, we cannot bring anything out of his house. But the moment he is bound in the name of the Lord, then you can spoil his house and his goods.

We all know that we are up against principalities and powers. The point is that the decree of God's throne has got to be carried into effect before anything can happen. The word of faith has got to be said in the place of prayer over the matter. Now that cannot be said easily. There has to come a point in our time of prayer where faith is manifested by the Spirit of God and, in that moment, someone breaks the sound barrier and utters witness to it. At that moment, something can happen. God help us if there is no such manifestation of the Spirit of God. We are lost because it means that we can cry and cry and cry, and plead and plead and plead; but until faith is given to actually mouth the very will and decree of God as if the thing is done here on earth, heaven will not do a single thing. Even though we have evangelistic meetings; we have children's work; we have teaching times; we feel that we are up against a brick wall, speaking against a brazen wall. There is teaching, teaching, teaching; and still there is no building up, there is no integration, there is no relatedness. Why? It is because there are principalities and powers that are sitting on the whole thing and they will not go until they are told that they are bound in the name of the Lord, until the word is said that the building work of Christ is released. But when the word is said in faith and it is supported by other members of the body, the work goes on.

So don't sit back and think, 'It is all right, we will come through; God is sovereign.' Why has every movement of the Spirit of God gone into death? Why hasn't the Lord sovereignly kept the Methodist revival alive, and the Puritan revival, the Quaker revival, the Brethren and the Pentecostal revivals? Why has he let it all die? It is because no one was prepared to listen to what God was trying to say at a point of crisis.

We may well ask why the Lord requires us to use the keys since he is sovereign. The only answer seems to be that he is training us all for eternal service in his kingdom. We shall never learn to exercise authority while he carries us. It seems to be a principle with God that he will not do anything until first we find out what his will is and then, in the secret place of prayer, speak of it as done. When that happens, God steps in and does it. We may think that everything now is the important thing. It is not with God. God is, in fact, training us for eternal vocation.

Using the keys

Declare the facts

Using the keys consists of three things. The first thing is declaring the will of God and the facts over a matter. In other words, when we have come to the clear conclusion together that the Lord is going to dislodge whatever it is, we say, 'This thing is dislodged in the name of the Lord. We have driven it out. The Lord is here. He has taken this place'—or whatever it is we are thinking about.

Behind the Ranges is the amazing biography of Fraser of Lisu land. After many years, Fraser finally got to the animist Lisu tribe in southwest China. They were demon-possessed; they worshipped spirits. He was the only believer in that whole area, ranging over hundreds of miles. He sought to do everything he could in that time to bring the gospel to those people. Not only did he not succeed, he himself, in the end, was unable to pray. He said it was as if an iron hand physically took hold of his throat and he was unable to get the words of prayer out. This happened day after day, and he wrote home: 'Pray, pray, I cannot get through. The powers of darkness are so tremendous here.' In those days, it took months for letters to get from China to the prayer groups that supported him.

One day, he read in the Scriptures that God has gone up with a shout and that God reigneth. Suddenly, into his head it said, 'Shout to the Lord with the voice of triumph.' So he decided to go up onto the highest peak in Lisu land. He climbed that peak and, turning to the south, he shouted, 'Jesus Christ is Lord of Lisu land!' Then, turning to the north, he shouted the same thing, and to the east, and to the west. When he came down, the power of that enemy had been broken. He was able to pray again for the first time.

All the prayer in the world did not do that. It was executive action. He did not even pray. He went up on the top and he declared something. In that moment, the keys were used and the powers of darkness in Lisu land were locked up. Within weeks, the first family of the Lisu turned to the Lord Jesus; then another family, then another. Just a few years ago, after all the suffering of

the Lisu people and the people who laid down their lives
to bring the gospel to them, including Fraser, the Bible
was finally published completely in Lisu.

It all came out of executive action. Supposing Fraser of
Lisu land had never climbed that mountain, and had never
declared the fact of the matter—that Jesus Christ is Lord
of Lisu land. All of the circumstances were against him;
all the evidence shouted to the contrary; but he declared
the fact. In that instant, it happened. So declare the will of
God and the facts.

Possess in the name of the Lord

Use the keys and possess the situation in the name of the
Lord. Take it. This may involve us in binding things or
loosing things, but we have to take the situation in the
name of the Lord. We have to possess it in the name of the
Lord.

Praise and worship the Lord

Now here we come to an aspect of executive action which
is very, very real but is often overlooked—that executive
action is a matter of worship. In no other aspect of prayer
ministry has worship such an integral part than in executive action. How do you really use the keys? You not only
declare the fact, you not only possess it in the name of the
Lord, but you start to worship the Lord and praise him, as
if the whole thing is actually, literally done. Actually it is
done in the unseen but it is yet to be carried out in the
seen.

The best example of this is King Jehoshaphat in
2 Chronicles 20 when they were surrounded by all those
enemies, a great confederacy of evil, and everything
seemed to be hopeless. They were blockaded. They
sought the Lord—supplication; they inquired of the

Lord, and the Lord spoke to them through a prophet. It was a manifestation of the Spirit. And the prophet said: 'Listen, all of you; don't fear, the Lord is with you. You do not need to fight in this battle. Take your position and stand still and see the salvation of the Lord. Tomorrow, go out against them. You shall find them at such and such a place.'

Now where did Jehoshaphat finally use the keys? At that point they all worshipped the Lord, but they did not really use the keys until the next morning. Early in the morning, when the army was ready to go out, Jehoshaphat and his counsellors had a conference, and evidently Jehoshaphat must have said to them, 'How do we express our faith in concrete terms?' And they must have had a talk about it. Finally, they said, 'We will put the choir in front of the army.' And you would have thought the choir would have sung a very militant song: 'He is Lord; our enemies have been defeated; they are under the feet of our Lord' or something like that. But no; they sang the most amazingly peaceful song, as if there was not even the scent of war in the air. They sang, 'For the mercy of the Lord endureth for ever.' They went out into the battle just as if they were having a Sunday school picnic! One side sang, 'For the mercy of the Lord endureth for ever,' and the other side sang, 'The mercy of the Lord endureth for ever. The mercy of the Lord endureth for ever. The mercy of the Lord endureth for ever.' And when they began to sing, the Lord sent liers-in-wait against the armies of Ammon and others, and they all began to kill each other (see 2 Chronicles 20:22); but it was only when they began to sing. That was using the keys, wasn't it? When the choir finally got there, not a single soul was alive. The whole place was littered with dead bodies, and there was plenty of spoil of all kinds. It took them three whole days to collect everything and bring it back to Jerusalem. It was a tremendous triumph.

There is one last point on this matter. Often, some further positive and concrete action has to be taken, and that is where I think we often fail. If we have prayed for someone's healing, and we are clear that the Lord has spoken to us about this person, it may well be that we should then go and pray for them in the name of the Lord. Sometimes, a concrete action has to be taken. It may be the sending of a sum of money. It may be moving in faith before we have the money we need. Sometimes we have to take positive action before the Lord supplies our need.

Practical points

How do we execute the will of God in prayer? These are a few things that may help you practically.

First, we are to take our place in Christ. Put on the whole armour of God. You should do this always in all times of prayer. But when there is going to be the possibility of executive prayer, then every one of us must consciously, deliberately, by faith, put on the whole armour of God; that is, take our position in Christ. That is where God has put us.

We must abide there (see Ephesians 6:10–18). We stand in him. We do not go back; we do not go forward. We do not do anything but stand, withstand, and having done all, stand.

Remember that we execute the will of God by standing. Be careful about being drawn out by the enemy and uncovered. That is a very real danger. He tries to get you to come out and get uncovered. Be careful; always remain hidden in the Lord. The victory is ours as we stand in Christ.

Second, we must have a knowledge of his will in the matter before us. You can never take executive action until you are quite clear as to what the will of God is in that matter. 'Do not be foolish, but understand what the will of the Lord is' (Ephesians 5:17 NASB). That is why this matter is so serious. It is utter nonsense for members of the body of Christ to say, 'We are too young; we do not understand; we do not know what the will of the Lord is.' The word of God to you is, 'Don't be foolish, but understand what the will of the Lord is.' God is far more interested in you knowing what his will is. We are being fools when we hide behind some smoke screen saying, 'I cannot detect what the will of God is.' It is your business to find out. You will never get into the eternal service of God unless you do.

Third, we must open our hearts and beings to the fullness of the Holy Spirit. We need to be filled with him so that we are full of faith, power, grace and wisdom. 'Be not drunk with wine, wherein is excess; but be filled with the Spirit' (Ephesians 5:18). Why do we not take executive action in prayer? It is because we are not filled with the Spirit. People just cannot rise to it. They cannot get there because, through devices of the enemy, they are not filled. Nevertheless, there is no excuse because our being filled is not a question of zeal, not a question of goodness, not a question of good works; it is a question of the grace of God and the finished work of the Lord Jesus Christ.

Fourth, we must be agreed together by the Spirit (see Matthew 18:19). We cannot take action until there is real agreement that this is the way, and then we must use the keys. One of the more responsible ones among us, by the Spirit, will do this. We need to be together and to second him. In other words, it is no good for someone to try to use the keys unless others are really with him in this matter. It has to be seconded.

Fifth, never enter into conversation with the devil, calling him names or deriding him. Remember that even the archangel Michael did not bring a railing accusation against him but said, 'The Lord rebuke thee, Satan.' If the archangel Michael was only able to say that, we too ought to be very, very careful. Do not think that you can call the devil names and get away with it.

I remember years ago, there was a particular situation among us over a sister who was undoubtedly in very, very great distress. One younger brother got carried away. He did not know too much about the fear of the Lord and he began to call the devil all kinds of names: 'You slimy serpent, you liar, you this, you that!' Some of us trembled for that brother. We could not even pray afterwards. All we could do was appeal to the Lord in our hearts to cover him. A curtain fell on him that night and he never recovered until about eight years later when the Lord graciously restored him. In those years, he was as dead spiritually as it is possible to be; and it came down that night. Never think that you can enter into conversation with the devil or deride him.

Sixth, see that you are right with the Lord before the prayer time begins, or we waste valuable time. Sometimes, people do not seem to get right with the Lord before the gathering. They do not bow their heads and say, 'Now Lord, if there has been any uncleanness or any defilement, I put it under the blood of the Lamb. I take my position in thee as my righteousness.' Instead, we find that some of the most valuable time is taken up by people saying, 'O Lord, we are so unworthy; I am so unworthy, I do feel a need, please do this.' It is quite humble; but it is much better to get that right with the Lord before we enter into the time of prayer. That is why in the old days among evangelicals, people used to get there a little before time and sit there not talking but getting right with the Lord. Maybe you did not realise that is why peole in the old days used to go in and sit there with their heads bowed in chapels. They were getting right with the Lord, so when the time began, they were all ready. That is an important point. If you are not right, this can contribute to heaviness and difficulty in the corporate time.

Seventh, if you are a woman, take real note of 1 Corinthians 11:10 where it speaks of having something on the head. Now, far be it from me to tell you what to do, but remember: 'The fear of the Lord is the beginning of wisdom.' I would have thought that one little phrase 'because of the angels' would be enough to make any woman sit up and take note. But you say, 'I do not understand it.' Yes, but the fear of the Lord is the beginning of wisdom. Or you say that it was an Old Testament custom; there are none of those customs today. What else was an Old Testament custom? Are you sure that our salvation was not an Old Testament custom? Where do we stop? What else do we throw out?

I am saying this simply because you may get away with it, even in a time of prayer; but when executive action is taken in prayer, we have to be very careful because principalities, powers, world-rulers of darkness, hosts of wicked spirits are all involved. So take that to heart and ask the Lord about it.

Last, we execute the will of God by declaring positive facts, ignoring Satan, and praising God. Sometimes, the way through in executive action is just to praise the Lord as if Satan is not even in sight, just like Jehoshaphat did. You would not have thought when they were going out into the wilderness that there was a great military confederacy waiting there to destroy the whole nation and take the city. They just ignored it. They did not even mention Satan. All they said was, 'The mercy of the Lord endureth for ever.'

7

Hindrances in Prayer

And not holding the Head, from which all the body by having nourishment ministered and knit joints and bands together, increaseth with the increase of God (Colossians 2:19).

Why is our prayer hindered so often when we meet together as the people of God? I am not referring here to those occasions when there is little petition or few words in a time of prayer, but when nothing really happens.

The Laodicean Church undoubtedly rumbled on after our Lord's word to it (Revelation 3:16). I suspect they had their Bible studies, their outreach, their times around the Lord's table, their prayer meetings, their Bible teaching, and all the rest of it. It would have been only those who were very alive to the Lord and sensitive to the Spirit of God who would have seen that the lampstand had gone. The thing just went on outwardly as it always had done, but the anointing had departed and with it had gone the testimony of Jesus.

This is a general principle of the church. This is not just to do with prayer at all. It is to do with our standing in Christ—that as we hold fast the Head, then we discover the body. You never discover the body by trying to hold fast the body. If we try to hold fast the body, the whole

127

matter of the church—its nature, the teachings concerning it, the truth that is contained in it—we will all go off the rails. Every single movement of the Spirit of God which has gone off the rails has, in fact, adopted this principle whereby we all sort of hold to one another. We hold to a teaching instead of holding fast the Head. When every member holds fast the Head, then we discover the body.

I believe that corporate prayer illustrates this principle perhaps more than any other aspect of the life of God's people, because you can tell in the time of prayer just how healthy the body is. If it is functioning, if there really is an anointing, if there is harmony and cohesion, if there really is direction going out to the body and through the body for the increase of the whole from the Head, you see it more clearly in prayer than in any other time. It is because the whole principle of corporate prayer is mutuality or togetherness. We are one body in Christ. We belong to Christ and to one another and, therefore, our times of corporate prayer are to be the expression of the burden, the mind, the will, and the design of the Head.

A prayer time is not just a time when we come with our own little burdens and petitions and we all do our own little bit—and having done our duty, we feel relieved. A time of prayer is really an expression of the one Spirit indwelling all the members of the body and transmitting to them all the burden and the will of the Head.

That is what it means in those verses that we have quoted again and again in Matthew 18:19–20. 'Again I say unto you, That if two of you shall agree on earth as touching any thing they shall ask it shall be done for them of my Father which is in heaven.' What a promise! This agreement comes, as we have seen, out of the risen Lord in the midst of us transmitting his burden, his mind, his will by his Spirit to the members of his body because they have gathered into his name. We are in his body; and as we are agreed by the Spirit, then those burdens, which really are the burdens of our risen Head, come out through our lips. When they come out through our lips and there is that witness in the mouth of more than two, then heaven moves.

Prayer becomes a thrilling thing when it is like that. There is a 'supply' referred to in the scripture at the start of this chapter—'being supplied and knit together'. There is no need to be afraid in a time of prayer when the enemy is sitting on us or twisting our corporate arm, as it were, up our back, or nearly pulling our leg out of joint. 'We wrestle not against flesh and blood.' If we hold fast the Head, there is a supply; there is equipment; there are gifts. There is a manifestation of the Spirit which can be given to us which can keep us on course, keep us specific, keep the edge of our prayers sharp.

As much as we may learn in prayer through the years, we must still say that sometimes the edge is so blunted. We go rumbling on and on because we do not see that we are a body. We are not just so many little individuals uttering our own things, but we are under the direction of the Spirit of God so that the risen Head can make known his mind. If you see that it is a matter of being one body in Christ, an expression of our risen Head through the Spirit, then the whole object of Satan is to paralyse the effectiveness of that prayer time by destroying our connection with the Lord and with one another.

Unforgiveness

The first hindrance in prayer I want to mention is unforgiveness. Whoever you are, whatever background you have, however wonderfully you have been saved, however marvellously you have been anointed with the Spirit of God, if you have unforgiveness in your heart, your prayer does not mean a single thing. It does not go beyond the ceiling.

> For if ye forgive men their trespasses, your heavenly Father will also forgive you. But if ye forgive not men their trespasses, neither will your Father forgive your trespasses (Matthew 6:14–15).

In other words, there is a blockage; God holds back. You cannot say, 'Oh no; surely not.' *God said this.*

Do you know that every time we have the record of the pattern prayer given, it was this that the Lord Jesus emphasised, not the other tremendous matters in that prayer such as 'Thy kingdom come, thy will be done, as in heaven so on earth'; or 'Give us this day our daily bread'?

Notice that he says *men*—that is, people generally. It is not a question of just forgiving believers. He did not say, 'If you do not forgive your brothers and sisters, neither will your heavenly Father forgive you.' He said, 'If you forgive not men.' That means the world. If there is someone we cannot forgive or will not forgive, our prayer life is destroyed. There is a shadow on it from the very beginning.

Some people feel their parents did them injury and they have bitterness towards them; it hinders prayer, and it hinders corporate prayer life. Notice how our Lord puts it first in the positive and then in the negative: 'If ye forgive men their trespasses, your heavenly Father will also forgive you. But if ye forgive not men their trespasses, neither will your Father forgive you.' Could the Lord make it more clear?

Let us consider the three realms of world, church and family. If there is someone in the world whom we are not forgiving, our prayer life is going to be hindered; and since we are members of one body of Christ, we hinder the whole. There may be people in the church you cannot get along with, so you think, 'I am going to leave: I cannot bear them.' You come here or go somewhere else and you say, 'Oh, I feel so happy here.' It is not for long because when you have had trouble somewhere else, before long, you will have trouble here. You carry your problems with you; like Jacob who ran away to Laban, and then got Laban for twenty-one years. The fact of the matter is that you never lose your problems. You carry them with you because, essentially, they are inside.

Now I realise there may be people who have problems with you and you have done every single thing to be right with them. There comes a point when you can do no more than walk before God. But it takes two to make division. When Peter said, 'How many times shall I forgive?' Jesus said, 'Seventy times seven.' That is how much you should forgive. Perhaps some of you feel you have already done that; but I want to remind you that when our Lord said that, he meant infinite fullness of forgiveness. He took the figure seven and multiplied it and said, 'Infinite forgiveness; there is no end to it.'

Unforgiveness, or an unforgiving spirit in any single member of the body of Christ, will paralyse the effectiveness of our corporate prayer; not only unforgiveness for the church and the world but for the family. There are many, many problems in families. Two people do not just live together. Even people who love each other cannot just live together all that easily. What a lot of forgiveness there has to be! What a lot of understanding there has to be! An unforgiving spirit destroys, but a forgiving spirit brings you into a deeper union with your Lord. Every time you forgive you are just like your Lord. It is as if you and he get together more closely than ever. He says, 'This is me in you.' Every time you lay down your rights, just surrender everything and press on, and you will find that you have more of the Lord.

Unconfessed sin

'If I regard iniquity in my heart, the Lord will not hear' (Psalm 66:18). Oh, how wonderful it is that we have such a salvation that all our sin can be forgiven; but unconfessed sin is not cleared. David knew very much about the forgiveness of God, and he said in one place, 'While I hid it in my heart, my bones burned' (see Psalm 32:3).

We have got to bring sin out into the open and get rid of it. But where there is sin in the camp, it is like the things Achan buried under his tent (see Joshua 7); only God sees it, but it brings about the defeat of the whole people of God. The whole nation was defeated because of unconfessed sin. It not only has to be confessed, but it has to be renounced; and when it is confessed and renounced, then there is a clear way with the Lord.

Unbelief

> For indeed we have had good news preached to us, just as they also: but the word They heard did not profit them, because it was not united by faith in those who heard (Hebrews 4:2).

There can come a point where we just don't believe, and sadly this happens again and again in prayer. We are facing some problem, and sometimes our hearts just do not rise to the situation. We are praying for some large issue and we say, 'Oh no, it can never be.' Or maybe we are praying for healing for someone and just because we have been in touch with one or two who have not been healed, we begin to get a kind of almost cynical approach. Whatever it may be, we have here an evil heart of unbelief. Let me remind you that when the church prayed, Peter was released by the ministry of an angel and James went out to have his head chopped off (Acts 12:2, 7). Do you think there were no angels with James? I think James had a thousand angels. Peter only had one, but Peter's one angel was obviously visible. James' thousand were invisible, but they supported him right through his martyrdom and brought him with an abundant entrance into the kingdom of God.

We might say, 'What went wrong with our faith? There we were in the upper room, praying our knees off, taking hold of the Lord; and then Peter got out and James got beheaded. How come an angel went and got Peter out and not James?' Some people come out with the most marvellous stories, and others have been martyred. But one day, when the whole story is told, those who went to their martyrdom or apparently never knew an answer to their appeal to God will have as great a story of the triumph of faith as those who apparently saw tremendous miracles. When we fail to remember this, we can fall prey to an evil heart of unbelief.

We can spend an hour of prayer with lots of words being spoken during this time, but if there is an evil heart of unbelief, the time is effectively paralysed. That is where we need this manifestation of the Spirit in the gift of faith. What a wonderful thing it is when someone prays with the gift of faith during a time of prayer when we were all feeling a bit heavy. Suddenly someone comes in with faith. Then we find our hearts lifted up, when it really is the Spirit of God and not just sentiment. We find something in us that says, 'Yes, that is right'; and immediately, we are out of our own unbelief.

So often this evil heart of unbelief is in the leadership. The enemy knows exactly where to get us. We who know the most can often be the most cynical because we are always having problems brought to us from all over the place; and after a while, we begin to wonder, 'Does anything ever happen?' And then, thank God, it does happen.

That is why we need each other. You see, we all have the idea that if God is going to do anything, he will only do it through leaders. The more responsible you are, then the more God will do. But sometimes the responsible people are the heaviest weight of all in any prayer time!

I could tell you about many times in the past where people have come to us and said, 'You know, while we were praying, I thought so and so'; and they had hit it right on the head. They had never been to a university or to a college. They were very simple, but they had got hold of something; they had a word of wisdom or a word of knowledge. They actually had the key to the whole situation. Then you suddenly remember that the Lord has tempered the body so that those parts that seem to be more important are, in fact, absolutely dependent upon those parts of the body which do not seem to be very important.

Husband–wife relationships

I think it is interesting that the word of God should centre on husband and wife relationships, but I suppose it is because, so often, it is in living together that so many of our problems come.

> Ye husbands, dwell with [your wives] according to knowledge, giving honour unto the wife, as unto the weaker vessel, and as being heirs together of the grace of life; that your prayers be not hindered (1 Peter 3:7).

What does it mean: 'according to knowledge'? Knowledge is the facts; therefore, you dwell with your wives according to the facts. I suppose that means that there must be times when you have got to show a lot of understanding. If your wife is a volatile person, that is one of the facts. So dwell with her according to that fact. If your wife happens to be more phlegmatic, accept that fact—according to knowledge, according to understanding. It is her position in the Lord. The Lord has received her, so you must receive her.

'Giving honour unto the woman, as unto the weaker vessel.' There is no women's lib here. You cannot argue with the Scripture. I have to say, as in all things, one has to take it by faith, because some ladies appear to me to be anything but the weaker vessel—physically, mentally, spiritually. Some of them appear to be extremely strong; but the word of God says 'as unto the weaker vessel'. It simply means that the lady is built on a different principle from the man. The fact of the matter is that even though men and women are equal in the sight of God—of equal value, equal in ministry, complementary—yet they are entirely different in the principles upon which they are built, both mentally and physically.

The Scripture is very clear about the place of women and their function as ruling the household, so men should not put their nose in the matter of ruling the household. The Scripture says a good wife should rule her household. In Proverbs 31, it speaks about the blessed wife and how marvellous she is. She buys and sells a field. (Some husbands would not hear of it.) She spins, goes down and sells it. She gets in a bit of cash on the side and carpets the whole house. No wonder many wives feel like dying when they see this ideal in Proverbs 31.

But if believers had only been taught what the Scripture has to say about the function of the wife, there would be no problem. It is because of this awful, twisted, evil thing that has come in that makes a woman some kind of chattel.

There is no such thing in the Scripture as a woman being a chattel. 'Male and female created he them, in the image of God.' That is the first word on this matter in the Bible.

The point is that the woman is the weaker vessel and the man is to honour her as the weaker vessel, she being a joint-heir of the grace of God. So no man can say, 'Look here, I am the one who gives life. I am the one who is the source of life.' It says 'joint-heirs'. After all, any woman with sense ought to come back on that and say, 'You would not be here but for a woman.' The fact of the matter is that we are 'joint-heirs' of life.

'That your prayers be not hindered.' I believe in these days in which we are living, in which family life is being subjected to such an onslaught from every angle, we need to protect the families in our midst. Every husband, every wife ought to get together before the Lord every day. There ought to be some 'family altar' where both of you worship the Lord and where problems can be sorted out 'that your prayers be not hindered'. It always takes two to create a problem, and it hinders prayer.

Disharmony

The other thing that hinders corporate prayer is disharmony, and I suppose we are all subject to that.

> Only conduct yourselves in a manner worthy of the gospel of Christ: so that, whether I come and see you or remain absent, I may hear of you that you are standing firm in one spirit, with one mind striving together for the faith of the gospel (Philippians 1:27 NASB).

This is interesting because it not only says *one spirit* but *one mind*. Now if it is difficult for us to take the position that we are one spirit, which is our position in the Lord— we are one body in Christ, by the one Spirit we have all been baptised into one body—how much more difficult is it for us to be of one mind? It is there that all the disharmonies come. It is there that all the cross currents begin.

It often starts with the silliest little things you could ever imagine. People become irritated with one another, old wounds get opened up, something is done, something is said; and before you know where you are, there are so many cross currents that the Holy Spirit has to spend three-quarters of the time trying to sort out the cross currents, right while we are seeking the Lord about some important matter.

We need to take our position in the Lord, to hold fast the Head. We cannot hold fast the Head and not then get into a right relationship with one another.

May the Lord help us in these things because prayer is not a devotional exercise. Prayer is a strategic and vital ministry of the church of God; and if the enemy can come in and by one means or another undermine the effectiveness of that ministry, he has in fact won the major battle for the life of that church. Before long, that whole company of God's children will come into ever more serious problems because the evil one has paralysed the effectiveness of corporate prayer.

May the Lord himself teach us in this area, so that we may know something of what it is to hold fast the Head from whom the whole body is joined.

8

Intercession
Part 1: The Mystery

For Zion's sake will I not hold my peace, and for Jerusalem's sake I will not rest, until the righteousness thereof go forth as brightness, and the salvation thereof as a lamp that burneth. And the Gentiles shall see thy righteousness, and all kings thy glory: and thou shalt be called by a new name, which the mouth of the Lord shall name. Thou shalt also be a crown of glory in the hand of the Lord, and a royal diadem in the hand of thy God. Thou shalt no more be termed Forsaken; neither shalt thy land any more be termed Desolate: but thou shall be called Hephzi-bah [My delight is in her], *and thy land Beulah: for the Lord delighteth in thee, and thy land shall be married. For as a young man marrieth a virgin, so shall thy sons marry thee: and as the bridegroom rejoiceth over the bride, so shall thy God rejoice over thee* (Isaiah 62:1–5).

In Isaiah 62, the one who speaks is not the prophet Isaiah but it is the word of the Lord in the mouth of the prophet Isaiah. In other words, it is the Lord who is speaking quite directly from the very beginning to the end of this chapter. If we understand that, it suddenly makes the whole chapter clear. It is the Lord who is speaking, and in verses 1–5, the Lord declares what is his sovereign purpose and his own determination for that purpose of his to be fulfilled.

Beulah is from the word that has to do with husbands. *Baal* means 'lord' or 'husband'. So you get this word

Beulah, meaning 'married'. You have got a husband—that is the thought in it. You are no more desolate or lonely but you belong; you are married. You belong to someone. What a wonderful purpose we have.

And then we have our responsibility in verses 6–7.

> I have set watchmen upon thy walls, O Jerusalem; they shall never hold their peace day nor night: ye that are the Lord's remembrancers, take ye no rest, and give him no rest (RAV).

In this one chapter we have the whole mystery of intercession. The Lord says, 'I will not hold my peace, I will not rest;' and then he says, 'I have set watchmen upon thy walls . . . they shall never hold their peace . . . take ye no rest and give him no rest.' There is a mystery. 'Ye that are the Lord's remembrancers'—what a wonderful word that is! If we meditate and reflect upon it, that one phrase should lead us to the whole secret of prayer: 'Ye that are the Lord's remembrancers.' We are not trying to persuade God to do something that he does not want to do. He has already declared his purpose, but we are the Lord's remembrancers.

Then we have in the next two verses (8–9) a further promise, and it is a very wonderful one:

> The Lord hath sworn by his right hand, and by the arm of his strength, Surely I will no more give thy corn to be meat for thine enemies; and the sons of the stranger shall not drink thy wine, for the which thou hast laboured: but they that have gathered it shall eat it, and praise the Lord; and they that have brought it together shall drink it in the courts of my holiness.

In other words, the produce of these servants of the Lord, these redeemed ones of God, shall not be dissipated or go to the wrong source. Isn't it tragic, when we labour so much and yet, in the end, enemies take what we have laboured for and foreigners or aliens drink our new wine?

Here is the promise of the Lord. If you understand the secret of intercession and give yourselves to that ministry of intercession, no matter what the cost, then the Lord gives a promise: 'that you shall no more be called Forsaken or Desolate but you shall be called, "My delight is in you", and "You are married, you belong to Me".' But more, the promise of the Lord is that what you produce through the grace of God and the activity of the Holy Spirit, you shall enjoy. It shall not be taken away from you, but you shall enjoy it. You shall see a harvest, you shall see an increase: 'They that have gathered it shall eat it, and praise the Lord.' There will not only be the weeping to begin with, connected with the sowing, but there will be the joy of bringing in a harvest.

Then in the last few verses, we have the practical meaning of all the Lord is seeking to say in this extraordinary chapter.

> Go through, go through the gates; prepare ye the way of the people; cast up, cast up the highway; gather out the stones; lift up a standard for the people (verse 10).

We have here an extraordinary commentary on true intercession. What do we do in intercession? We go through the gates. The Lord said: 'Upon this rock I will build my church; and the gates of hell shall not prevail against it. I will give unto thee the keys of the kingdom of heaven' (see Matthew 16:18–19). We said that here we have three things: the kingdom of heaven, the gates of hell, and the building work of our Lord Jesus. And unless you and I are prepared to take the keys of the kingdom of heaven and lock up the gates of hell, then the counsels of hell will prevail against the building work of the Lord Jesus. And unless there are times when we take the keys of the kingdom of heaven and unlock the gates of hell so that those captives of darkness may come out into his marvellous light, we shall never see the building material for the house of God.

The whole thing is summed up here in intercession: 'Go through, go through the gates.' It is not just that we should indulge in evangelism, but rather we should learn in the secret place how to intercede by taking no rest and giving the Lord no rest, by being his remembrancers. So often we dither over so many of the matters that come up in prayer because we do not know any direction from the Lord. We are all following—ring through nose—instead of being sensitive and alert to the Holy Spirit. We do not go through the gates. We dither and dither instead of going through the gates.

'Prepare the way of the people.' A people are coming for the Lord that are locked up by the gates of hell. They are coming for the Lord. Prepare the way for this people; and you prepare it in prayer.

'Cast up a highway.' Did you ever see one of those big motorways being built? You will see, instantly, the amount of work that is entailed in casting up a highway. It is no good just preparing a way for the people; it has got to be actually produced. It has to be 'cast up'. Whether it goes through mountains, over obstacles, over rivers, wherever it is, somehow or other, this highway has got to be made. There has got to be a casting up of the highway.

'Gather out the stones.' Now these days we have bulldozers and many other mechanical means of removing enormous boulders from the way; but in the old days, some of those enormous rocks, especially in mountainous countries such as Israel, were real problems to road builders. And you have only got to see some of these so-called roads to wonder how people ever walk up them without breaking their ankles, especially after the winter when the rains and snow have been at work. The thing seems almost impossible. I remember looking at one of these so-called roads in Samaria, and wondering how anyone could ever walk up such a road. It was not even a pebbled way. To call it a road was quite extraordinary.

There are so many things that are stumbling blocks: devices of Satan, works of Satan, all these things that lie in the path of people who would come into God's family and into the kingdom of our Lord Jesus Christ. There are so many things that would trip them up. They are works of the enemy; and our job in intercession is to gather out the stones and to lift up a standard for the peoples. It is to show the flag; and that has something to do with executive prayer.

The vital need of genuine intercession

Wherever we look, we see on all sides of us the most terrible and dire need. We see the deterioration of national character; we see the breakup of morality, of ethical standards. On every side we see the inroads of not just a new ideology; we see the inroads of darkness. We see before our eyes the battle being fought for the soul of a nation. It is incredible to me that the people of God can go along to their dear little meetings and sing their sweet hymns and twitter away as if they are in a paradise when they are teetering on the brink of tragedy. And wherever we look, on all sides, we see this dire need in our land.

We see it in all the nations of the West. I suppose there is hardly a nation in the so-called free world where this need is not apparent. Everywhere, the powers of darkness are at work and the battle is being fought for the destiny of the nations. Now that is not just political or economic, but behind the whole thing lie principalities, powers, world-rulers of this darkness, hosts of wicked spirits in heavenly places. Behind it all lie those strongholds, those satanic

fortresses—imaginations, speculations, high things
exalted against the knowledge of God; thoughts that
seem so innocuous to begin with, but in the end emerge
to capture millions of human beings and blind them to the
truth of the gospel.

When we look at our country, it is not only the deterioration and the breakdown that we see, but we see a
blood-guiltiness spreading all over the country. Take, for
example, the matter of abortion. It is a theological problem. Where does human life begin? The Bible says that
the Lord puts the spirit into a life within its mother's
womb. Where then does that person become a human
being; and where does it incur murder when it is
aborted? If that is true, our land is covered with blood-
guiltiness; and nation after nation in the free world is
following in this pathway. Now I am not talking about
those times when there is a need, medically, for abortion,
but about 'abortion on demand'. And if that disregard for
God-given life goes on, in the end it must incur the wrath
of God, for God is the creator and producer of all life.

That is only one aspect of a problem, a dire need that we
see on every side of us. We see the hovering judgement of
God upon the nations of the West. Is there a nation upon
which the hand of God is not hovering in judgement?
There must be very few indeed in the free world over
which the judgement of God is not already beginning to
gather.

And if that is what we may call the political, economic,
or moral need, what about the spiritual need of the church
of God in the midst of the nations? If we do not see the
vital need of intercession when it comes to the nations of
the world, surely we must see the need for intercession for
the work of the Lord in building the church of God, in
producing the bride of the Lamb. Do we think that that
work is just going to go on willy-nilly? Do we think,

somehow or other, without any co-operation on our part, that that work will be fulfilled? What does Isaiah 62 mean when the Lord says, 'For Zion's sake will I not hold my peace, and for Jerusalem's sake I will not rest, until the righteousness thereof go forth as brightness'? It is not only for the earthly Jerusalem and the earthly Israel, and the earthly land that the Lord will not rest, but the Lord has a consuming passion for the calling out of a people for himself from every tongue and kindred and nation on this planet.

Surely we see a tremendous need when we see the church of God in the midst of the nations. We find so much weakness, confusion, division and compromise even where the Spirit of the Lord has come and touched and renewed. Oh, the need there is all over the world! If we were to confine ourselves just to those who have known renewal, there alone there is a colossal need for intercession. The enemy is coming in on all sides; the powers of the air are seizing upon all that the Lord has started to do.

There are many Christians who tell me that the people of Britain are a hopeless lot. They are cold, hard, indifferent, pleasure lovers, money grabbers, swindlers; and all they are interested in now is higher wages and fewer working hours. Britain is finished. Does the key, therefore, lie in some kind of mass movement on the part of the whole British people, or among the peoples of the free world to turn to the Lord in sufficient numbers and somehow or other get blessing? Of course, that would be true if they did; but where does the key lie to the situation?

Others will say that the key to the situation lies with the church of God, the whole mass of saved men and women—that if only we were all filled with the Spirit, if only we were all renewed, then things would happen. Does the key lie, then, with the great majority of the redeemed?

It lies with none of these. The key lies with the intercessor. And this is why you and I have such a solemn
responsibility to face in the presence of God because the
key to this national situation does not lie with the British
people and does not even lie with the church of God in
Britain in general, but it lies with the intercessor.

> And the Lord saw it, and it displeased him that there was no
> judgment. And he saw that there was no man, and wondered
> that there was no intercessor: therefore his arm brought
> salvation unto him; and his righteousness, it sustained him
> (Isaiah 59:15b–16).

> And there is none that calleth upon thy name, that stirreth up
> himself to take hold of thee; for thou hast hid thy face from
> us, and hast consumed us because of our iniquities (Isaiah
> 64:7).

The prophet Isaiah says that the final judgement is when
there is no intercessor. That is the ultimate judgement of
God upon any nation—when there is not even an intercessor.

In Ezekiel 22, we have this terrible description of a
country that is departed from God. Every single part of
her, including those who are servants of the Lord, have
departed from the Lord; and then come these remarkable
words:

> And I sought for a man among them, that should make up the
> hedge, and stand in the gap before me for the land, that I
> should not destroy it: but I found none. Therefore have I
> poured out mine indignation upon them; I have consumed
> them with the fire of my wrath (verses 30–31a).

Notice that word 'therefore'. 'I sought for a man . . . I
found none. Therefore have I poured out mine indignation
upon them.' The key to the whole situation was a man
who would stand in the breach, a man who would build up

the wall, who would somehow stop the whole flood of evil coming in over the land, who would plead with God; but there was none.

> Thus saith the Lord God, Woe unto the foolish prophets, that follow their own spirit, and have seen nothing! O Israel, thy prophets are like the foxes in the deserts. Ye have not gone up into the gaps [breaches], neither made up the hedge for the house of Israel to stand in the battle in the day of the Lord (Ezekiel 13:3–5).

The point is that the key to all these situations lies with the intercessor. God does not delight in judgement. So many of us have this heathen, pagan idea of God that he is a being with a terrible and dark propensity for destruction, that he loves judgement; and if there is any tipping of the scales, he will always tip in favour of judgement rather than mercy. This idea is found in nearly all of us in some form or other, and so often it destroys our relationship with the Lord. The Lord does not delight in judgement. He is not some cold, impersonal being; some divine all-knowing, all-powerful machinery. God is a Person and it pains him whenever he judges. Now if we could get hold of that fact, it would explain everything. Yes, he is a God of judgement. But the fact is this, that because he is love, he never judges without pain.

That is why you have these incredible passages in the word of God when it seems as if God cries out. In one place, he says, 'I cry out like a woman in travail; but you will not listen to me.' It is hard for people to believe that God could ever go berserk—and that would be almost blasphemous to suggest—but there are passages where the force of this is brought out in a really modern version, like the Living Bible, where it seems as if God is almost out of his mind, where he cries out to people to listen, but they are heedless.

You have it in the words of the Lord Jesus, God manifest in the flesh, when he said, 'O Jerusalem, Jerusalem, thou that killest the prophets, and stonest them which are sent unto thee, how often would I have gathered thy children together, even as a hen gathereth her chickens under her wings, and ye would not!' (Matthew 23:37). And he was weeping. It is incredible to me, therefore, that we should think that God can judge a Babylon, a Nineveh, or some great area of the earth without even a feeling. There are Christians who can sit down and eat a steak when 20,000 people have been destroyed in an earthquake. And in one way, I do not wholly blame them because, just because 20,000 people have died on the other side of the world, we cannot take them all on ourselves. Otherwise, none of us would eat anything. But God is not like human beings. Not a single sparrow falls to the ground without God feeling it (Matthew 10:29). How much more then does he feel every time something happens to a human being into whom God has breathed an eternal soul?

Do we really believe that God can issue judgement with a flick of his hand, like some oriental potentate, or like Henry VIII saying, 'Off with their heads!' Some people's idea of God is just like that. But God loves people.

The great shock of Jonah's life was to find out that God loved Nineveh, that he knew all about the domestic animals in Nineveh, and all the toddlers who could not tell their left hand from their right. Jonah never thought that God had any time for Nineveh. Jonah thought: 'Now God loves Jerusalem; God dwells in Jerusalem; God knows every toddler in Jerusalem. He knows everyone who is in Jerusalem, even the most depraved he knows and loves and grieves over. But God has no time for Nineveh, that city of cruel, hateful Assyrian people. In the end, their day will come and he will judge them without so much as a feeling for them.' But when Jonah went with his message and the whole city of Nineveh, from the royal house down to the animals, was clothed in sackcloth and ashes, God delighted to show mercy and deferred judgement upon them for one whole generation. It is true that judgement came in the end, but for a whole generation it was deferred.

Jonah could not take it. He stomped out of the city in a deep sulk and all he could do every time the Lord came near him was spit and hiss. And God prepared a gourd that grew up within a night, and as the first rays of the rising sun fell on it, God prepared a worm. Unbeknown to dear Jonah, who so appreciated the gourd that grew up in just a few hours, the worm would destroy the gourd in a few hours. And God prepared a sultry east wind that made poor Jonah so weary of life altogether. It was then that God said to him, 'Jonah, you almost wept tears over that gourd that grew up in a day and died in a day; yet you do not think that I should have mercy upon a city in which there are one hundred and twenty thousand toddlers who cannot even tell their left hand from their right, and domestic animals?'

Only a great man could have left the story of Jonah where it is left and not added that further paragraph that I certainly would have added, that Jonah saw the error of his ways and became a man full of love ever after. He left it where every preacher can talk about the hardness of Jonah, even though Jonah was broken and saw the purpose of God for Israel.

But don't we have to say that we are just the same? We do not have that heart for certain situations or for certain peoples. God never judges a city or a nation or even a system without grief. He always looks for an intercessor— even just one intercessor who will stand, at whatever cost, in the gap; who will build up the wall against the enemy;

who will plead from a broken heart. There are very few occasions when God has ever found such an intercessor.

Do you remember Abraham and Sodom and Gomorrah? Have you ever asked yourself why the Lord had that extraordinary conversation with his friend Abraham?

In Genesis 18, it says that the Lord said to himself, 'Shall I withhold from my friend Abraham what I am going to do to the cities of the plain, to Sodom and Gomorrah? No, I will go down and I will speak with him.' Why did the Lord do this thing? Surely, we would argue, if the sins of the cities of the plain have reached a certain standard, then judgement must surely come. Why go talk with Abraham about it? Of course, Abraham had his relative, his nephew Lot, down there. Maybe it was that.

But it was much more than that. God was training Abraham for eternal vocation; and if I may put it like this, there was almost a twinkle in the eye of God when he went to Abraham and said, 'Abraham, I feel I should not withhold this from you, that I am going to judge the cities of the plain.' And then God just waited. He knew exactly what Abraham was going to do because he was finding a reflection of his own character in Abraham.

Immediately, Abraham said, 'Don't be angry, Lord, but just supposing there are fifty righteous people in those cities. Wouldn't you spare them?'

And the Lord said, 'If there are fifty righteous people, of course I will spare them.'

Then Abraham said, 'Don't be angry, I will speak again; suppose there are only forty-five?'

And the Lord said, 'Yes, if there are only forty-five, I will spare them.'

And so it went on, down to ten. The Lord was loving Abraham every moment they got down to a lower number, because what he saw in Abraham was himself. God did not want to judge the cities of the plain. He did not want to do it. He sought for a man to stand in the gap and he found one.

It was tragic that Abraham did not go on after ten. But he stopped; and there were not ten righteous people in the cities of the plain. Why did God go through all that with Abraham? It was because God had pain in his heart about judging even Sodom and Gomorrah. If there was the possibility of deferring judgement, it would be deferred.

You have the same thing with Moses in Exodus 32. The people had all been murmuring and worshipping the golden calf. And the Lord said to Moses, 'Moses, they have all gone after some Egyptian idol.' Moses was sad and the Lord said to him, 'Stand back, stand back, I am going to destroy the whole lot; I will make an end to this whole nation—all their murmuring and criticising and all the rest of it. Stand back, Moses. I am going down there to destroy the whole, and I will make of you a great nation.'

Now, many of us in the same position would say, 'Well, of course, I am one of the remnant. Yes, that sounds good. They are a difficult lot. Maybe you should put an end to them, Lord, and start again with me. If they were all like me, we would not have any trouble.' Many of us would have argued for this. The way God put it was to draw out from Moses any self-principle that was in the man, any pride; but Moses was of a different ilk altogether. What he said was, 'No Lord; you cannot do this thing. What will the nations say? If they find that you have brought out all this people only to destroy them all, they will think you are capricious.' Later on, in the last verses of the same chapter, you find that when it seemed that the whole nation would be destroyed, Moses went before the Lord and said, 'Lord, forgive this people. Forgive them.' He pleaded with the Lord to forgive them, and then he said, 'If not, Lord, blot me out of your book.' The Lord saw in

Moses the very character of his Son, that says, 'Blot me
out, but save them.'

What a solemn responsibility, therefore, rests upon all
of us, both individually and corporately. This is not just a
study; you may be sorry you've read this because, even if
you are half asleep, the word of the Lord has still come
and you cannot get away from it. The solemn responsibility is a challenge to every single one of us. It is not the
British people that are the key to the situation, nor the
peoples of other nations, nor even the church of God in the
midst of this nation or in the other nations; the key is the
intercessor.

The nature of true intercession

Now we will consider the nature of true intercession.
There is an idea that intercession is just locking yourself
away for a few moments and uttering a few prayers for
some situation on the other side of the earth or somewhere
in this country. Of course intercession, in its simplest and
its most shallow form, must involve such prayer; but
intercession is far more than prayer—even pleading,
fervent prayer. It involves your whole being—spirit,
soul and body—and it identifies you not only with God
completely but with the people for whom you pray.

In other words, anyone who starts on this path of
intercession will find that they are becoming more and
more identified with God. They will find the cross! And
they will find that they have got to lay down their lives,
not once, but again and again, and every time more
painful. You cannot pray for others, you cannot intercede
for others except you become identified with the very
character of God who puts everyone else first and thinks
not of himself. You also become identified with the people
for whom you pray. Rees Howells discovered that it would

have been such an easy matter if he could just shut himself away in a room and say a few prayers, utter a few petitions, weep a few tears, and that was all there was to it. But he found out that God required his spirit, soul and body. It meant that God had a claim on every moment of his time, on all his energy, on every single thing that belonged to him; and in praying for others, there were times when he came into inexplicable situations where he was identified with the very people for whom he prayed. It is therefore, as you can see, a most costly and painful ministry.

In the book of Nehemiah, you find another example of true intercession (see 1:4–2:8). Nehemiah did not pray in some superior manner for all the rest. And this is one of the great problems with intercession. One of the real dangers of intercession is superiority. Unwittingly, because we are praying for others and for their needs, we begin to pray in a way as if we are above them and they are down there. The principle of intercession is that you are not only so identified with God but you become so identified with the people that you pray as if their sins are your sins.

Now Nehemiah had suffered to be in the king's house. It was no easy thing for him to be there in an uncompromised way. Yet it says in this great prayer: 'I pray for the sin of thy people Israel. We have sinned and done wickedly.' All the way through his prayer it is *we*. That is intercession.

You will also notice that he wept and mourned for many days. The king finally asked him why he was looking like that when he was not ill. He said, 'You must have great sorrow of heart.' That is intercession. This man was not just having some half-hour of intercession and then just floating out and enjoying himself. The burden of the Lord had so got into the man that it involved his whole being.

You find the same thing in Daniel 9; and when I read Daniel's great prayer in that chapter that got him into so much trouble, I begin to wonder if this is the same man who was so saintly, who paid such a price in order to be kosher in Daniel 1. It is hard to believe it is the same man because he said, 'Lord, we have rebelled against thee; we have done wickedly; we have broken thy commandments; we have dealt treacherously with thy law and thy covenant.' But Daniel had not. It had cost Daniel everything not to break the covenant. It had cost Daniel everything to keep the commandments of the law; but here he was praying as if he were the worst sinner of them all. That is intercession.

Intercession is far deeper than words or petitions or even tears. There are those who believe that if you can weep in the place of prayer, that is intercession. But I believe that sometimes the greatest intercession of all is so painful that you cannot even weep tears. It is the travail of the Holy Spirit in and through us. In Romans 8:26–27, we read these amazing words:

> Likewise the Spirit also helpeth our infirmities: for we know not what we should pray for as we ought; but the Spirit itself maketh intercession for us with groanings which cannot be uttered; And he that searcheth the hearts knoweth what is the mind of the Spirit, because he maketh intercession for the saints according to the will of God.

Some people say that when you hear someone groaning in a prayer meeting, that is this ministry. I remember years ago going to a place where there was a person who continually groaned very much like a cow in a field! Every now and then, you heard this strange sound; and I was told by someone afterwards that this person had the ministry of groanings which cannot be uttered. I thought that was extraordinary since it is called groanings which cannot be uttered—inaudible groanings.

Intercession is when something is conceived in you so deep in your own spirit that it cannot come out; it cannot be communicated, not only in your own language but not even in a tongue; it cannot even be communicated through groanings but is something imprisoned within you. It says, 'The Spirit itself maketh intercession for us with groanings which cannot be uttered.' And it says that this intercession for the saints is according to the will of God.

What an extraordinary thing that you and I can have something conceived in us by the Holy Spirit that we cannot even communicate in words of any kind, which is the Spirit himself travailing in us. In other words, our spoken ministry of intercession is like the tip of an iceberg; it is only an eighth above the water. The greatest part is hidden.

The apostle Paul said, 'My little children, of whom I travail in birth again until Christ be [fully] formed in you' (Galatians 4:19). Note that word 'again'. Evidently, he travailed before for them to bring them to Christ.

Oh, don't we fail? Some of us have spent time in agonising prayer and anguish that men and women would be saved, but who prays for the full formation of Christ in those who have been saved? That really is the building of the house of God—the full formation of Christ; our being fitly framed together, knit together; growing up into him as Head, through whom the whole body finds its position and function.

Dear child of God, what a responsibility is ours! We could see many more people saved if we knew something more of this travail. The very word 'travail' speaks of the pains of childbirth. They are not enjoyable pains, but they are all part of a process which ends in new life.

Psalm 126 speaks about the Lord turning again our

captivity as the streams in the south. Now the streams in
the south, in the Negev, can be dried-up river beds for
almost twelve months of the year. Then suddenly, without
warning, the cloudburst will come and the rivers will be
full of water for just a day or two. 'Turn again our
captivity as the streams in the south.' We would love,
sometimes, to see something happening, bit by bit; to
see it all building up: 'We are getting nearer; we are
getting encouraged.' But Psalm 126 gives us no encouragement right up to the moment of the cloudburst. Sometimes, there will be some river beds that are never filled
with water for four or five years. And it is quite unpre-
dictable just where the cloudburst might come. But the
Lord goes on to say in Psalm 126 that those who sow in
tears shall reap in joy.

I was with my 'Auntie Smith' one day who said to me,
'Now we are going to be joined by two other missionaries
this afternoon, and we are going to have a time of intercession. Would you like to join us?' I said 'yes', not
knowing how to read the twinkle in her eye. Now I
knew these two knew all about intercession, but I was
totally unprepared for the time that we had. The time
went on quite all right until, suddenly, one of these dear
ladies, who appeared to be a perfectly normal lady, started
praying. For five minutes she prayed, punctuated with
sniffs and sobs in a high falsetto quavering note. And
then almost as suddenly as it had begun, she said, 'In
the name of the Lord Jesus Christ.' And she stopped,
and she was normal. Of course, I was young and irreverent. I kept my eyes wide open and looked at her for some
time, and when they had gone, I said to Auntie, 'Could
you tell me, what was that lady doing?' She said, 'She
believes that she is fulfilling Psalm 126: "Those that sow
in tears shall reap in joy."' And she put the accent on *she
believes*. And I said to Auntie: 'Who is she kidding? Did

she really think that God was taken in by that?' Now some people cannot help crying in prayer; it is a normal thing for them. God bless them. But when people suddenly turn on the sniffles and sobs because they think they are fulfilling a promise and they are sowing in tears, whom are they kidding? The devil himself must have a laugh at it. It is a waste of time. If a real anguish came into that person's heart, they would probably hardly be able to say a word.

This kind of intercession will involve us in all kinds of experiences and circumstances which would not normally come our way. If you have started on the path of intercession, look out. You will find that the Lord will lead you into the most extraordinary situations, into things that will come your way just because you are an intercessor.

Do you remember Ezekiel? He was an intercessor; he stood in the gap. And it was the result of Ezekiel's ministry, along with Daniel's, that the people went back to the land in the end. But it cost him a very happy marriage. One day, when he was praying, the Lord said to him: 'Your wife will die today. You shall not mourn; you shall not cry because it is a sign. You shall go out and say to the whole city, "As my wife has died, so will this whole city die"' (see Ezekiel 24:15–24). You may find that a very strange thing for God to do. But there are some even stranger things in the word that God has led intercessors into.

Intercession will introduce us to the fellowship of Christ's sufferings in a very real way. Paul said in Philippians 3:10: 'That I may know him, and the power of his resurrection, and the fellowship of his sufferings, being made conformable unto his death.' In no other sphere are we introduced to the fellowship of Christ's sufferings as we are in the realm of intercession.

I believe that this is what the apostle Paul meant when he said these mysterious words:

Who now rejoice in my sufferings for you, and fill up that
which is behind of the afflictions of Christ in my flesh for his
body's sake, which is the church (Colossians 1:24).

Intercession, therefore, results from a burden conceived
in us by the Spirit of which the audibly expressed words
are but the smallest fraction. One of our great problems
when we know something about intercession is that we
find it all locked up inside, just like an unborn baby. There
is something within our very being which is alive, something which has life within, something conceived by the
Spirit of God; and yet we are unable to communicate.
Such is this ministry of intercession.

The mystery of intercession

If God is sovereign and works all things according to the
counsel of his own will, why the need for intercession? I
think we face here the mystery of intercession. I have
often pointed out to you how Daniel saw something that
many modern believers do not recognise. In Daniel 9:1–2
it says quite clearly that by the words of the prophet
Jeremiah, Daniel understood that the seventy years of
captivity were over. Then he did that which so few
modern believers, under the New Covenant, ever dream
of doing. On the basis of that revelation by the Spirit of
God as to the meaning of the word of the Lord to the
prophet Jeremiah, he got down on his knees and began to
fast and mourn and seek the Lord and confess the sin of
the whole people and intercede for them that they might
go back to the land. Now most of us would say, 'He is
wasting his breath; the Lord has already said that they are
going back. Why start praying if the Lord has revealed
through the prophet Jeremiah that after seventy years the
people are going to go back?' But Daniel knew that this

sovereign decree and purpose of God had to be ratified in some way on earth by servants of the living God. So he started his ministry.

Now many Christians have told me at different times when we have started praying about different things: 'I think you are just wasting your time, wearing yourself out. You do not need to pray for such things.' Hell, by contrast, understood only too well the significance of Daniel's prayer ministry. For if you compare the date in Daniel 9:1 with Daniel 5:31, you will discover that when Daniel was thrown into the lions' den coincided with his prayer ministry in Daniel 9. In other words, hell became so disturbed by Daniel's prayer ministry, the word went out: 'It has got to be stopped!' One thing I am always thankful to the Lord for is that hell does not know everything. We tend to think that the devil is like God, a counterpart of God, and that he knows everything; he is everywhere at the same time. He is not. He is a created being, and he can only be in one place at one time. And being a created being, although he has great intelligence, he is nothing like God. He has limited intelligence. (I do not mean that in a rude way, but he has limited intelligence in the sense that I have got far, far more limited intelligence!) And I believe that when he put that thought into the other principals to go to the king, Darius, and get that decree passed that no one should pray except to the king, they thought it was the end of the ministry.

Daniel could have said: 'Now I must not be a fool. The law has been passed. It is according to the law of the Medes and the Persians, and it does not alter. I must not be a fool. After all, what is one month? I will just stop praying for a month. Then after a month, I will take it up again. Why stir up the whole opposition?' But Daniel was such a different type of person. He got something from the

Lord by the Spirit of God through the word of God, and he knew that the priority was to pray that thing into being.

Dear old Daniel must have battled it out with his conscience as to whether he should have rendered to Caesar what was Caesar's or to God what was God's, until finally, he flung the shutters open at the appointed time of prayer, knowing full well that they were all watching him, and continued with his prayer ministry. Of course, he ended in the lions' den; but he never stopped his prayer ministry. He only spent one night in the lions' den and they were like purring cats. He came out after one night and all the opposition went in and were eaten by the purring cats! And we believe Daniel overlived the return to Jerusalem by at least three years, though as far as we know, he never returned himself.

We are face to face with a mystery here. Why does God require someone to pray into being something which he has already said is going to come to pass? You work it out. Anyone who thinks they understand prayer does not know how to pray. I have said at all the schools of prayer, wherever I have been, that you will never learn to really pray until you face the mystery of prayer. If you conduct prayer as a science, God help you. The fact is that prayer is a mystery.

In some strange way, out from the throne of God and into my heart by the Spirit of God has got to come the burden that is on the heart of my Lord. It comes into my heart by the Spirit of God, it comes out of my lips by the Spirit of God—just a fraction of the burden—and it finally goes back to the throne of God and is accomplished. It is like a full circle. And then the thing is done. I can only believe that God wants us to be one with him. In some strange way, he says, 'Here is my will. If you do not do it, I will not.' After all, God does not have to do it. We seem to think that God has got some great self-interest in doing it. He does not have to. He will just say, 'Well, if you do not want to, I will not.'

People say to me, 'I cannot understand. It says, "Upon this rock I will build my church; and the gates of hell shall not prevail against it." But they have.' It is because people have not used the keys. God says, 'If you do not use the keys, the gates of hell will prevail.' In other words, God is training us. There comes a time when you cannot carry a person any more; they will never learn to walk. You have got to put them down and let them walk. And so it is with us. It is practical union with Christ which gives rise to all true intercession. In some way, beyond our human comprehension, the intercession of Christ over-spills into us. And so that intercession is really the expression—a very faint expression—of the intercession of the Lord Jesus at the right hand of God. It is the most wonderful way to look at intercession. My Lord, at the right hand of God, has a burden, and in some wonderful way, a little faint reflection of that burden gets into me and comes out of my lips and involves my whole being in the fulfilment of the purposes of God.

9

Intercession
Part 2: The Sacrifice

Finally, my brethren, be strong in the Lord, and in the power of his might. Put on the whole armour of God, that ye may be able to stand against the wiles of the devil. For we wrestle not against flesh and blood, but against principalities, against powers, against the rulers of the darkness of this world, against spiritual wickedness in high places. Wherefore take unto you the whole armour of God, that ye may be able to withstand in the evil day, and having done all, to stand. Stand therefore, having your loins girt about with truth, and having on the breastplate of righteousness; and your feet shod with the preparation of the gospel of peace; Above all, taking the shield of faith, wherewith ye shall be able to quench all the fiery darts of the wicked. And take the helmet of salvation, and the sword of the Spirit, which is the word of God: Praying always with all prayer and supplication in the Spirit, and watching thereunto with all perseverance and supplication for all saints (Ephesians 6:10–18).

And I sought for a man among them, that should make up the hedge, and stand in the gap before me for the land, that I should not destroy it: but I found none. Therefore have I poured out mine indignation upon them; I have consumed them with the fire of my wrath: their own way have I recompensed upon their heads, saith the Lord God (Ezekiel 22:30–31).

What does God require for intercession? If we want to be intercessors, part of a company, if we want to know what it is not only to make supplications and prayers and thanksgivings but also intercession, what is it the Lord looks for? When you look around, both globally and locally, there are a thousand and one pressing needs for true intercession. So what is it that the Lord requires in a person or company who will intercede?

Here we come to the crux of the whole matter; indeed, if it is possible so to speak, it is here that we find the divine dilemma. I do not know whether it is even correct theologically to speak of God having a dilemma. God can do all things and is all-sufficient; yet in one sense, from the human point of view, in this whole matter of intercession and the thing that qualifies an individual to be an intercessor or any company to be intercessors, there is a divine dilemma.

Babes cannot travail; children cannot travail. The paramount need, if anyone is going to know something of travail for birth, is adulthood, even if it is minimal adulthood. There must be a certain, essential minimum maturity before anyone can know anything about travail. Now this is absolutely true of the church, for intercession is travail.

I have pointed out that intercession involves your whole being. Sometimes, true intercession will bring you into situations where it is impossible to put the whole thing into words. And when you do put it into words, it only adds to your pain because you are so conscious that you are unable to communicate the real pain or the real burden that has been conceived and born in your heart.

But if intercession requires adulthood, we have to face the simple fact that the church of God is full of babies. Some of them are seventy, eighty years of age, but they are babies, spiritually. If we could only say before God that this great number of babies was the result of a great movement of the Spirit of God which had swept thousands of new ones into the kingdom of God, what a joy it would be. But we cannot say that. What we have to say is that the church of God is made up of a large majority who have never moved beyond spiritual babyhood. That is the divine dilemma. They are not even children, for the most part. The vast majority of believers should have spiritually grown up long ago, but they are still spiritual babes.

Now there is nothing wrong with babyhood at the right time—there is not a person alive who has not been a baby—but there is everything wrong with it if it is prolonged. What happens to a mother if she suddenly finds that her child's babyhood is prolonged? It should cause her very real concern and worry, because prolonged babyhood is unhealthy. And if it becomes quite clear that the child is not going to grow any more, then there is something seriously, radically wrong. Modern Christianity, for the most part, is unhealthy because it is built not on laying down your life for the Lord and for others but on what you can get.

Now the principle of babyhood is that a baby is only interested in what it can get. All the time, it only thinks of food, or of being cuddled, or of having rattles or dummies or toys, or of people cooing. And there is nothing wrong with that. But if a child grows up to be eight, nine, ten years of age and all they could think about is what they can get, there is something very wrong indeed.

When we are first saved, God takes care of us in the most wonderful way. We only have to cry and he is there to cuddle us. We only have to wail and we get a rattle or a dummy. He feeds us every time he feels it is right to feed us, and it is quite regular. The Lord really takes care of us when we are babies. But for the most part, we Christians do not grow out of that babyhood stage; and the tragedy is, we glorify it as if it is something that belongs to Christianity. Then our whole gospel becomes something of what you get instead of what you give. The whole thing becomes a question of everything revolving around you; it is for your benefit.

Of course the Lord, in his infinite mercy, knows that we are all self-centred. He loves us so much that there is not one of us who would be saved or in the kingdom if he had not played a little on our self-centredness. Do you know a single person who has ever really been born of God and truly converted who came to the Lord because they loved the Lord their God with all their soul, all their heart, and all their might? I don't. I have gone all over the world, and I have never met a single person yet. I would love to meet someone who came to the Lord just because they loved the Lord.

I find that all of us came either through fear of death, or fear of disease, or fear of living, or fear of problems, or through emptiness, or misery, or circumstances that were hopeless. And the Lord was so gracious. He said: 'You are dead, I am life. Come to me and I will give you life. You are unsaved; I will save you if you come to me. You are neurotic, you are restless; you come to me, I will give you peace. You have no joy, you are miserable; come to me and I will give you joy. You are going to hell; come to me and I will give you heaven.' It is surely the great love of God that he never just simply said, 'Unless you are prepared to love me, I will not save you. Unless you show absolute love towards me that is total, I will not save you.' No, he loves us so much that he was prepared to get us.

Now in our babyhood stage, the Lord puts up with all this self-centredness. But there comes a point when he starts to deal with us, and that makes all the difference between growing from childhood to adolescence and to adulthood. We have often thought even of gifts and an experience of the Holy Spirit in a totally self-centred way. People want to be satisfied. It is not that people want to serve others or want to serve God or want to get over their problems that they may glorify God, but rather it is, 'Give me, give me, give me; I want, I want.' Now that is a sign of babyhood; and when we all look at ourselves, we have to say, 'Oh, I am found out,' because there is hardly one of us who does not fall unwittingly into this category.

Spiritual maturity is not that you are perfect, but it begins when you go over from the self-centred principle to the Christ-centred principle. In other words, there comes a point, which can be so painful that at the time it may appear to be almost total destruction of your being, where you move over from what you get to what God gets. From then on, it is not your joy, it is his joy that counts; not your satisfaction, but his; not your will, but his; not your increase, but his. From then on, it is only what is the Lord's that matters. That is the beginning of spiritual maturity.

No one can intercede until they are prepared, first, to sacrifice themselves. And that is the point I am seeking to make. In other words, there is no such thing as intercession in our babyhood stage, because we could give half an hour to it and we would feel good for it. You know the kind of thing—'I have given half an hour to the Lord.' We feel so terribly good about it. Or we even fast for a day and we feel so good at the end. It is just a bolstering of what we are. We really quite enjoy it because we feel we have done the Lord good and the work of God good, and we have helped things along a little. But that is not real intercession. Real intercession is that your whole time, your money, your energy, your life, your future, your prospects, your everything are taken into the hand of God. It is up to him what he does with you.

Do you think that Ezekiel enjoyed the day his wife died? Do you think it was easy for Hosea to go down into the slave market and choose a prostitute for a wife? Do you think it was easy for some of these men to live through the kind of experiences they had in order to become, as it were, those who built up the wall and stood in the gap? Do you think it was easy for Joseph to go down into Egypt and into the dungeon of Pharaoh until the iron entered into his soul? Do you think it was easy for him after having a dream about everything bowing down to him—all the sheaves bowing down to him and the stars bowing down to him? In the end, it seemed like a mockery until the iron entered his soul and he no longer bothered about anyone bowing down to him, only that he belonged to God and that he was with God. Then he became an intercessor, and then God took him out of the dungeon and up and up until he became the supreme power of one of the greatest empires of the world. He became a true intercessor, by whom not only Egypt was saved but Israel as well.

So it is all the way through the Book. You find that only when people are prepared to lay down their lives in totality can they become intercessors in the real meaning of the word. God gets right into them and involves them in a situation in such a union and identification with himself that he can touch situations substantially, materially, and indeed, in some cases, eternally.

Until we are prepared to lay down our lives, we cannot intercede. You can give an hour and feel the better for it; you can give a day and feel the better for it; you can give a week and feel the better for it; but to give a lifetime is the question. If God can get a lifetime for himself, then he can save a nation, he can touch situations all over the globe.

Rees Howells was the illustration of this principle. He taught us that a humble miner's son, in the end, could be taken up by the hand of God and used to deliver not only the British Isles but a whole continent from Nazism. He taught us that once God can get hold of a body—not just a man's spirit but his body—then he can start to do things in this world.

Rees Howells had his faults and his failings, and there are many who will speak about them but I remind all of those people who love to point out the flies in the ointment that maybe they themselves would not be there but for Rees Howells. Did they ever give themselves to months and months of prayer? Were they ever wakened in the middle of the night so that they spent days in anguish for a nation? Never!

The interesting thing about Rees Howells is that he put things very crudely, and when I first read him, I could not take it. It seemed to me to be the antithesis of all that is spiritual. I can understand why people sometimes criticise Rees Howells because what I heard him say was: 'What God wants is your spirit. He wants your heart, and when he has got your heart, he has got you.' But what Rees Howells said was this: 'When the Holy Spirit looks for an intercessor, he looks for a body: ''Give me your body. I want your body: I want your eyes; I want your ears; I want your mouth; I want your feet; I want your hands; I want your heart. I want your body so that I may feel things through you, think through you, react through you. I want to use you in such a way that the other situations for which you are going to intercede will influence you, will make you feel, will touch you, will pain you.'' '

How can anyone possibly know anything about genuine intercession if their life is not laid down? When they give an hour, that requires a little bit of sacrifice, but it really isn't anything, is it?—one hour out of twenty-four hours;

one hour a week? Quite honestly, what is it? But when a life is laid down, then that person's time is the Lord's. It is not as if the Lord will trample over you all the time and simply treat you like dirt. God will give you back your time; but your time is his, your energy is his, your money is his, your being is his, your health is his. Every single thing about you is his.

Requirements for genuine intercession

A *living sacrifice*

Thus the Lord requires three things for genuine intercession. First, your body is to be a living sacrifice.

> I beseech you therefore, brethren, by the mercies of God, that ye present your bodies a living sacrifice, holy, acceptable unto God, which is your [spiritually intelligent worship] . . . but be ye transformed by the renewing of your mind, that ye may prove what is that good, and acceptable, and perfect, will of God (Romans 12:1–2b).

That is the first fundamental and essential requirement for true intercession. If you and I are not prepared to come to the place where our bodies are a living sacrifice, there will be no intercession. You will pray; you will supplicate; you will know worship; you will know blessing; you will see the Lord; but the Lord must say when he looks at the thousand and one situations: 'I sought for a man to stand in the gap and to build up the wall that I might not judge the land, but I found none.' Some people are prepared to pray; yes, but that is a little different. Being prepared to pray is one thing—and don't give up praying—but to stand in the gap may cost you your life. To build up the wall may cost you everything. That is another matter.

'Present your body a *living* sacrifice.' No sacrifice was ever dead. Any animal that was brought for sacrifice was alive and it had to be without spot or blemish, perfect. The priest went right through it folding back its fur to see that there was no spot or blemish. He looked behind its ears, looked in its teeth, and if it was perfect, he passed it. And only when it was passed did it become a sacrifice. And then it was consumed by fire. 'I beseech ye therefore, brethren, by the mercies of God, to present your bodies a living sacrifice.'

Spiritual maturity and capacity

> That we henceforth be no more children, tossed to and fro, and carried about with every wind of doctrine . . . but speaking the truth in love, may grow up into him in all things, which is the head, even Christ (Ephesians 4:14–15).

The second absolute essential for intercession is spiritual maturity and capacity. The Holy Spirit may long to use you, and when he sees a longing in your heart, the Holy Spirit loves you. He is not some hard-task schoolmaster. He just loves anyone who has the desire there, even though they do not have the capacity. Nevertheless, all the desire in the world will not create spiritual capacity, nor can it be created overnight. It is something which God has to do in us day in and day out, week in and week out, month in and month out, year in and year out. And then a spiritual capacity is produced in us, a spiritual maturity is produced in us. Then when the desire is there to serve the Lord in this way of intercession, the Holy Spirit can come and conceive a burden in you and develop it in you; and finally, he will enable you to fulfil that burden.

A progressive experience of the Holy Spirit and the cross

It is not enough in this matter of intercession to have had an experience of the Holy Spirit, nor is it enough to have had an experience of the cross; it must be progressive.

You may have known what it is to be baptised into the Spirit in a very real experience, but still not know anything about intercession today because you are not filled with the Holy Spirit. If you are not led by the Holy Spirit, if you do not walk by the Holy Spirit, if you are not filled by the Holy Spirit, if you are not anointed by the Holy Spirit in a fresh way, then you will never know what it is to intercede.

This is the same with the cross. Some of us may have had a real experience of the cross years ago. We laid down our lives, we made a covenant with the Lord, we saw something, we stepped forward in faith and God took us at our word; but unless we are prepared to lay down our lives again and again, there will be no intercession.

Now you may feel after reading all this that you cannot intercede in any way. Nevertheless, let me say this to your comfort. Everything begins with that initial presentation of our bodies as a living sacrifice. Don't let anything that I have written here make you feel that you can *never* intercede. If the desire is there, give yourself to God in a new way. Remember the old Chinese proverb: 'A journey of a thousand miles begins with one step.' Maybe God is calling on you to make an initial step. You do not know where it will lead you. It may be a journey of a thousand miles, but you will never reach the goal unless you first take the initial step. God will do the rest for you.

Corporate intercession

This matter of intercession is much more specifically related to individual spiritual growth and individual spiritual character than any of the other aspects of prayer. For example, supplication, thanksgiving, praise, and petition are not quite so related to individual growth, but intercession really does rest on individual spiritual capacity and individual spiritual character and growth.

Nevertheless, while there are great individual intercessors and, even more wonderfully, twos or threes that are bound together in intercession, there is nothing in the whole universe as powerful as corporate intercession. I believe that the devil has fought like fury to keep the people of God from ever coming to the place of corporate intercession. It is because he knows that in the moment the people of God come to the place of corporate intercession, all kinds of situations will be radically altered. Things can be touched in a way that nothing else will do. The keys of the kingdom of heaven can be used.

I believe that is one of the reasons why the devil hates any recovery of the church. Some people have got the idea that Satan hates any recovery of the nature of the church, the coming together of the people of God simply because Jesus said, 'Upon this rock I will build my church.' But in actual fact, even the church is a means to an end. It is to be the expression of Christ, a manifestation of Christ. And the most wonderful thing about being the body of the Lord is that the members are so related to the Head, so related to the one Spirit, that the burden of the Head can come into the members and all kinds of things can be done on earth by the risen, ascended and glorified Head.

Obviously not everyone in a church can be of the same spiritual maturity or capacity. Indeed, that is not what God requires. In any healthy company of God's people there will be all the different spiritual ages. There will be those who are spiritual babes, those who are spiritual children, those who are spiritual adolescents. You must have that in any healthy company of God's people. And, of course, I must say, as things lie at present and right to the very end, we shall have those who are babies long beyond babyhood stage and those whose spiritual growth has become deformed or somehow stunted. Nevertheless, the Lord will take the nucleus in that company and train and qualify them for corporate intercession. And if they are ready for it, all kinds of inexplicable personal and family situations will come to them to bring them to the place of spiritual capacity and spiritual maturity as quickly as the Lord can.

But in any company, there must be a nucleus of people who have laid down their lives and presented their bodies as a living sacrifice to God. Then that great work of qualifying them for intercession through educating them and training them begins. It will cost them everything. But even more wonderfully, once he has established it, the Lord will add to that nucleus all the time. It will be through the older ones and the way they pray, their character in prayer, the way they bear the holy things upon their shoulders that will, in the end, influence the younger ones and educate them and train them into the same ministry.

Sometimes, in the most marvellous ways, the Lord will take that whole church into the ministry of intercession and then the youngest in the church will benefit by it and will be part of the intercession. Now this is the lovely thing about corporate intercession, that even though those youngsters will not be able to feel the pain and know what it is to have something locked up inside, yet they will still be in the good of the intercession and indeed be part of it, just because it is a body thing now. Once God has got that nucleus, he can bring all the others into it.

I do not believe there has ever been a time in our history when we needed to know more about this matter of intercession and when we stand more seriously at the crossroads. None of us knows how long we have. But I do feel that the Holy Spirit would teach us, from the youngest to the eldest, something more about intercession.

An experience of intercession in Richmond, England

I would like to tell you a personal experience in this matter of intercession. In the beginning of August 1951, I and a few others were deeply burdened for the state of things. We felt, somehow or other, that with all the great evangelical paraphernalia we had around us, we were not really seeing people touched for the Lord locally nor were we seeing any real building work. To put it into words, which I could not have done then, God had no home in Richmond. He had plenty of believers and plenty of evangelical places of worship, but there seemed to be no home for the Lord.

Now at that time, all the talk was of the Hebrides revival. There were two old ladies who had spent six months in prayer every night until, in that most sovereign way, God poured out his Spirit upon the Hebrides. And there were seven old gentlemen on the other end of the island, unbeknown to the two sisters, who had met once a week for two years for a prolonged session of prayer to pray for the same moving of the Spirit of God upon those islands. Everyone talked about it at the time, hoping that this outpouring would come down south and that we would see something happening everywhere.

At the same time, I had read Charles Finney's *Lectures on Revival*. If you wish to be deeply disturbed, I recommend you read it, particularly the chapter on 'Plowing up the Fallow Ground'. I found myself very disturbed at that time, along with seven others who were burdened. We talked about it, not knowing whether this burden was a burden of God or whether it was emotional, subject to outside influences, not from the Lord.

So we covenanted together to do an extraordinary thing. We would not speak about revival, read about revival, pray about revival for one whole month; and if at the end of that one month this burden was still in us, we would know it was the Lord. And we covenanted to give ourselves to prayer until the Lord did something. So for the month of August 1951, we neither spoke about revival, nor read about it, nor prayed about it.

At the end of the month, we found that the burden in us was greater than ever. It was a pain. I was only a young Christian, but I can only describe it as an incurable pain. I could not get it out of my system. It was just there, like a deep, deep anguish of spirit.

On the first day of September we started to pray, and we prayed every evening up to Christmas. Our times of prayer began just after seven o'clock and went on until ten or ten-thirty. In the middle of it, we had the severest fog that London has ever known, in which three thousand people died. For ten days we could not see across the street. All transport stopped at one point and it was hopeless. But it never stopped our prayer. We walked every evening to those times of prayer. Sometimes, there were only two of us. We were never less than two and we were never more than eight; but we prayed every single night. We used to pray on Saturday afternoon from two o'clock until six o'clock so that we could go along to the young people's time in the evening. And we got permission to pray in the vestry of the church on Sunday evening so that we were not a faction or division, and we prayed for the service as well.

Now the incredible thing was that we did not know too much about prayer. I had learned some lessons in intercession in Egypt and I had seen a whole number of people saved whom God had put on my heart. It had cost me everything to pray for those. But I knew nothing of corporate intercession.

It was amazing that we had one simple burden and we never varied from that burden. It was not as if we prayed for Nepal or China or anywhere else; we prayed simply for Richmond and the Thames Valley. We prayed night after night for something like three hours—never less. I am amazed at it myself now. It is like a dream. But I remember that when we began, we could do nothing else but pray. At the end of those three hours, it was like a tank that had drained all of its water and one could get up quite relieved. But by the next morning the tank was full again. You just felt uncomfortable and unhappy, as if you had a pain inside, and the only way to let it out was prayer.

That was my first real experience of corporate intercession because it was the Spirit of God who was in us, keeping alive a burden. We prayed for nightclubs; we prayed for hospitals; we prayed for schools; we prayed for colleges. It is a very interesting thing that many of the schools that have seen blessing are the places we prayed for, night after night. Of course, we had no idea that one of the nightclubs we prayed for would be closed down by the police for immorality and we would actually get possession of it and meet there for one whole year. That would never have entered our heads when we were praying.

Those four months of prayer for the same thing were an incredible experience. We felt as if we were in some sovereign flow of God. You know how hard it is to pray for one subject for half an hour. We prayed for virtually one subject from all angles for three hours every single day right up to Christmas of 1951. Out of that came Koinonia, an interdenominational get-together of young people in the town, just to wait upon the Lord.

We had covenanted with the Lord that we would not stop praying until we saw two things—the unsaved in Richmond turning to the Lord, and the people of God renewed. We went on praying in 1952 for the first three weeks of January, but we could not go on any more. The burden lifted, and we could not understand it. We felt so terrible because we had covenanted with the Lord that we would pray until we saw these things happen, but never in our wildest moments did we think of Koinonia as an answer to our prayers. And because the Holy Spirit was in charge, we knew that we could not flog a dead horse. We found that it was no good just going on in prayer evening after evening. The whole anointing had gone from it. So we gave it over to the Lord and said, 'Lord, we leave it with you. You bring it back at the right time.'

In those very early days, from time to time, we had weeks of prayer which were tremendous times. And always we got the same promise—that in the end, God would do it—and we found the burden lifted. It was our experience of corporate intercession.

It is an amazing thing to me that exactly a decade later, in September 1961, we began to pray again with exactly the same burden. Leading up to that were studies on the book of Joel and the recognition that the prophecy on the day of Pentecost had not been exhausted on the day of Pentecost but has included the whole of the age in which we are found, right to its end. We had studies on the book of Jonah and were shocked to discover that God was as interested in Nineveh as he was in Jerusalem, and he knew the people of Nineveh as much as he knew the people of Jerusalem. Out of this, once again, came two burdens. One was that unsaved people would be saved in our area, and the second was that God would do something new in his people all over the country.

From 1951 to 1961 God led us, and we saw some very precious truths. But we were a shut-up company, ostracised. No one would touch us with a barge pole. We were the offscouring. We belonged to that most dreadful of all groups, Honour Oak; and anyone who was associated with Honour Oak was absolutely beyond the pale. 'Be careful of them. They have got some sort of spiritual infection that will touch others and destroy them.' So for all those ten years, hardly anyone ran the blockade and got into us except those whom God saved among us.

I went away in August 1961 and a dear brother said to the whole company at the time, 'Do you not feel that God is calling us to prayer? And if he is calling us to prayer, are we prepared to sacrifice everything that we may intercede?' And while I was away, they decided: 'Right, we will sacrifice everything. Every gathering will go by the board except the Lord's table and the Sunday evening gathering. Everything else will be prayer—every night, Monday to Saturday. We will meet every night for prayer, and we will take hold of the Lord, as he enables us, until something happens.'

The remarkable thing is no one recognised that it was ten years to the day that we started to pray. It was only a month afterwards that we suddenly realised we were back again on the old thing. Only this time, instead of praying for Richmond and the Thames Valley, we were praying for the whole of the British Isles. We prayed that the house of God would be built in the whole of the British Isles and that there would be a renewal that would sweep the people of God into a new way with the Lord.

We went right through one whole year and we never had a Bible study during that time. The amazing thing is that we began to see quite a few more people saved. We went into our second year and we did not have a Bible study for a second year. We went two years without a Bible study; and then we found that we had so many new ones saved, almost sort of unwittingly, that someone said, 'Don't you think they ought to be taught?' The only thing they were getting was prayer; and they were growing marvellously in prayer, but there was no actual teaching. So we brought back the Thursday Bible study.

So then we had Sunday and Thursday, and every other night was prayer. Now of course, by then some people thought we were crazy. They had always thought we were crazy outside the company, but some people inside the company thought we were crazy by then. I remember people coming to me and saying: 'I think all this prayer is ridiculous; it is destroying everybody. People are absolutely worn out. Where are we getting? We are getting nowhere.' But we had a burden in our heart that something had to be done, that something had to go through. We could not let it go, and we were very conscious of it ourselves: 'Are we flogging a dead horse? Here we are day in and day out, saying the same thing, taking hold of the Lord, and yet we cannot get away from it.'

I remember so well that Wednesday of the third year. It was the fewest we had ever been, about fifteen in all. None of the responsible folks were there. But that Wednesday was incredible. Oh, it was an oppressive time! Now this may be for the encouragement of you all because, so often, we feel when there is an oppression that there is something wrong, when in actual fact there may be something very, very right. When there is deep oppression that comes upon a company, you may be right on the brink of very real blessing.

I began to think, 'I am going to talk to the brothers as to whether we should really let this whole thing go. It is really silly, just fifteen of us.' And I remember that, suddenly, it was as if all of us looked into heaven—that is the only way to describe it—and the time became hilarious. We laughed. It was such a heavy dose; we were laughing, almost stupid with it all. Then a word came from the Lord: 'Within a year, the walls will come down.' And it was confirmed in other ways.

Of course, people thought we were praying for the locality. But we were praying for the whole country.

And the most interesting thing was that a while later we heard that down in Cornwall, the Spirit of God had been poured out on a group there. That was the first beginnings in our country of what has been called the charismatics. Then we heard reports of all these people speaking in tongues, and we were very suspicious of it. Everyone thought, 'That is not what we were praying for.' But I do remember (I thought it was so wonderful) that when we were praying, a brother said, 'Lord, we do not care what you do, we are even prepared to speak in tongues.'

Whatever our feeling was at the time, the walls did come down; and by the grace of God, they have never been put up again. Until that date, we were an ostracised company. From that date onwards, our ministry as a company extended to the ends of the country and, in many ways, all over the world, because God had started to do something which was irreversible. Whatever people may say about the charismatics, it has brought thousands into a new experience of the Lord. People who were dead, dry, old bones, whom you could not have fellowship with, not for all the tea in China, suddenly you met and found you could have fellowship with them. They were hungry for fellowship. They began to talk about being in the body. I remember one famous evangelist's wife saying to a mutual friend: 'I cannot understand Lance. All this talk about the body is so niggardly. When we are in heaven and see our Lord Jesus, it will all seem so silly and small.' But then we found people everywhere talking about the body, about being in the body of Christ.

In those days, if you met in a house or in a home, you were considered to be absolutely below par. There was something very suspicious about you. From then on, we began to find all over the country—in farmhouses, in homes, in cottages, in big beautiful houses—people were meeting in drawing rooms and lounges to worship the

Lord, to study the word, to seek God in prayer. I am not saying there were not great weaknesses and excesses and failings and so on, but the fact of the matter is that God was doing something which was irreversible.

The last year we spent every evening praising the Lord. I am not saying that it was hard to praise the Lord, but we praised the Lord that the walls were down, and it seemed so stupid. But the Lord said it, and so we said, 'We are going to praise him; we will not pray any more. We have spent three years in prayer, now we will praise the Lord.'

We must be very careful that we do not lose what God has given us in this matter. Intercession is the most hidden of all ministries. By its very nature, the laying down of a life is not a thing that's trumpeted. It is within a person's being or a company's being. For the most part, it is hidden.

There are few who are prepared to enter such a ministry of intercession. I believe that with all of our failings in this part of God's family, he has taught us something about intercession which has been, if I may so say it, incredibly precious to the Lord. I believe, also, that it is something which the devil hates and he will work unceasingly as we grow larger and become more popular and more in demand to take away and to undermine such a ministry. We need to hear the cry of God: 'I sought for a man to stand in the gap and to build the wall, but I found none. Therefore have I poured out my indignation upon the land.'

When I was a little boy, I remember being told a story that gripped me as a child. It was the story of a little Dutch boy of six or seven years of age who was playing away from home on the dikes of Holland that keep back the sea from flooding that low-lying country. While he was playing on those dikes, he suddenly heard the sound of running water; and when he looked down, he saw the sea coming through the hole. And he knew, though he was very young, that it meant death for thousands of people. He did not know what to do. So he did the only thing that came into his head; he put his arm in the hole. He was found dead the next day with his arm in the hole, but he had effectively plugged the breach. Thousands of people had been saved, but it had cost him his life.

I believe that story illustrates genuine intercession more beautifully than anything else I could say. 'I sought for a man to stand in the gap [or breach] and build up the wall, that I might not judge the land, but I found none.'

May God help us to be his remembrancers, who take no rest until God has spoken and acted, allowing our hearts to be melted, that we may truly know what it is to be a company who watch and pray.

The Uniqueness of Israel

by Lance Lambert

Israel. The Holy Land. There is no area of the world like it. Its language is a modern miracle. Its past is pivotal in understanding world history. Its chief city has a special role to play in international events.

But more important than all of this – and the key to a proper understanding of Israel's place in world events – is its Messiah: the Saviour of the world. For while much of Israel has rejected him, he has not rejected them, but intends to bring about their renewal and restoration before the close of the age.

This latest edition contains a new foreword by Ken Burnett of Prayer for Israel, and also the text of a prophecy which was given to Lance Lambert at the Intercessors International Conference in Jerusalem on 3rd November 1992.

 Kingsway Publications

Learning the Joy of prayer

by Larry Lea

You may know that praying to the Creator of the universe is your duty – a privilege, even; but can prayer be a time of great *joy* more than just once in a while?

At a crucial stage in Larry Lea's life, when he felt discouraged, he was drawn again to that most familiar of prayers, 'the Lord's prayer'. It took just twenty seconds to recite. But this time Larry felt God challenge him to pray it more slowly, reflectively. So began an exciting journey of discovery that turned his prayer life from drudgery to pure delight.

LARRY LEA is founder-pastor of the 7,000-strong Church on the Rock in Texas, with many thousands more having responded to its call to a life of commitment and prayer. *Learning the Joy of Prayer* reveals the ways in which prayer times can be turned into life-changing events.

Kingsway Publications

Pray in the Spirit

by Arthur Wallis

In this book Arthur Wallis concentrates on the ministry of the Holy Spirit in relation to prayer, and investigates the full meaning of the apostle's injunction to 'pray in the Spirit'.

He analyses the spiritual and practical difficulties we encounter, and shows how the Holy Spirit helps us in our weakness and makes up for all our deficiencies. We are encouraged to yield ourselves completely to Him allowing Him to pray through us.

As we enter into the 'deep things of God' unfolded here we shall discover a new power and effectiveness in our Christian lives.

Kingsway Publications